AF333889

ROBERT IRWIN Site Determined

ROBERT IRWIN Site Determined

Edited by
Matthew Simms

With essays by
Ed Schad
Matthew Simms
Sally Yard

CALIFORNIA STATE
UNIVERSITY LONG BEACH
ART
MUSEUM

DelMonico Books•Prestel
Munich London New York

This book was published on the occasion of the exhibition *Robert Irwin: Site Determined*, organized by the University Art Museum, California State University, Long Beach and curated by Dr. Matthew Simms.

Exhibition Itinerary:
University Art Museum,
California State University, Long Beach:
January 28, 2018 – April 15, 2018
Rubelle and Norman Schafler Gallery at the Pratt Institute School of Architecture:
September 1, 2018 – November 30, 2018

Published in 2018 by the University Art Museum, California State University, Long Beach, and DelMonico Books•Prestel

University Art Museum
California State University, Long Beach
1250 Bellflower Blvd.,
Long Beach, CA 90840

DelMonico Books, an imprint of Prestel,
a member of Verlagsgruppe Random House GmbH

Prestel Verlag
Neumarkter Strasse 28
81673 Munich

Prestel Publishing Ltd.
14–17 Wells Street
London W1T 3PD

Prestel Publishing
900 Broadway, Suite 603
New York, NY 10003

www.prestel.com

© 2018 University Art Museum, California State University Long Beach and Prestel Verlag,
Munich · London · New York

Editor: Matthew Simms
Authors: Matthew Simms, Sally Yard, Ed Schad
Designer: Andrew Byrom
Managing Editor: Maria Coltharp
Development Coordinator: Brian Trimble
Copy Editor: Ellen Thornton
Production Director: Karen Farquhar,
DelMonico Books•Prestel

Printed and bound in China

Library of Congress Cataloging-in-Publication Data

Names: Simms, Matthew Thomas. | Schad, Ed. | Yard, Sally. | California State University, Long Beach. University Art Museum, organizer, host institution.
Title: Robert Irwin : site determined / edited by Matthew Simms ; with essays by Ed Schad, Matthew Simms, Sally Yard.
Description: Long Beach : California State University ; New York : DelMonico Books/Prestel, 2018. | "This book was published on the occasion of the exhibition Robert Irwin: Site Determined, organized by the University Art Museum, California State University, Long Beach and curated by Dr. Matthew Simms." | Includes bibliographical references.
Identifiers: LCCN 2017034157 | ISBN 9783791356716 (hardback)
Subjects: LCSH: Irwin, Robert, 1928---Exhibitions. | BISAC: ART / Individual Artists / Monographs. | ART / Sculpture & Installation.
Classification: LCC N6537.I64 A4 2018 | DDC 700.92--dc23
LC record available at https://lccn.loc.gov/2017034157

ISBN: 978-3-7913-5671-6

A CIP catalogue record for this book is available from the British Library.

Foreword by
Kimberli Meyer

Robert Irwin: Site Determined, organized by the University Art Museum (UAM) at California State University, Long Beach (CSULB) and curated by Dr. Matthew Simms, explores a body of Irwin's work that is interdisciplinary in scope and bilingual in form. Irwin is a visual artist in dialogue with the canon of art, and as such, art is the primary language of this work. But architecture is a close second. Like architecture, Irwin's site-determined works are developed and communicated through drawings and models—abstractions that stand in for real-scale, real-material ideas. Like architecture, these works disrupt public space, introducing new circulation patterns and spatial modalities. And crucially, like architecture, Irwin's works are rooted in site, with site analysis and interpretation as their starting point. Given that every site carries its own specific and dynamic data, a fraction of which is visible at any given moment, what an artist or architect chooses to respond to is key to the meaning of the work.

The CSULB campus is a complex site. Its administrative environment is governmental and educational, the product of a public university system and the state of California. Its focus is on providing accessible higher education and encouraging upward economic mobility for an emerging citizenry. Its built environment is the result of a master plan designed by Long Beach architect Edward Killingsworth, a noted Case Study House Program architect. An elegant work of institutional mid-century Modernism, the campus is understated and generous with landscaping and public space. The university's historical environment includes Puvungna, the Native American village and spiritual center for the Gabrieleño and other local Native Americans. It's on the National Register of Historic Places and is an active Native American Graves Protection and Repatriation Act site. If one of the roles of cultural and artistic action is to uncover and highlight information from hidden strata, the CSULB site is rich with potential.

The originating work of *Robert Irwin: Site Determined* is *Window Wall* (1975), which was part of an exhibition entitled *A View Through*, organized by the Museum Studies Program and Art Galleries under the guidance of founding UAM Director Constance Glenn. The simple rectangular white plane fills one bay of a perimeter colonnade. A picture window-like void occupies its center. When it was first installed, the piece performed a disruption in public space, stopping the foot while directing the eye, playfully hijacking human movement and perception. Today, the work is almost stealth—to the uninformed or inattentive, it may pass as not art. Today, the work is almost stealth—to the uninformed or inattentive, it may pass as not art. This is partly because the work adopts the form of the modernist language of its surrounding architecture, and partly because the collective memory of its pre-existence has nearly lapsed. In Irwin's work, absence and presence have a complex and ever-shifting relationship.

I am grateful to Dr. Simms for his extensive scholarly work on Irwin and the knowledge he brings to the curatorial process. Special thanks go to the funders of the project, which include the Institute of Museum and Library Services, the Graham Foundation for Advanced Studies in the Fine Arts, the Pasadena Art Alliance, and the Contemporary Collectors-Orange County. Thanks to our *Window Wall* conservation partners Rosa Lowinger, the Getty Conservation Institute, and colleagues at Physical Planning and Facilities Management. I am grateful to the catalogue designer, Andrew Byrom, for his generosity, and to the UAM staff and student assistants for their unflagging enthusiasm and rigor. A very special thanks goes to Robert Irwin, for his support of the exhibition and for giving generations of students, faculty, and employees the daily opportunity to encounter his work and reflect upon their surroundings.

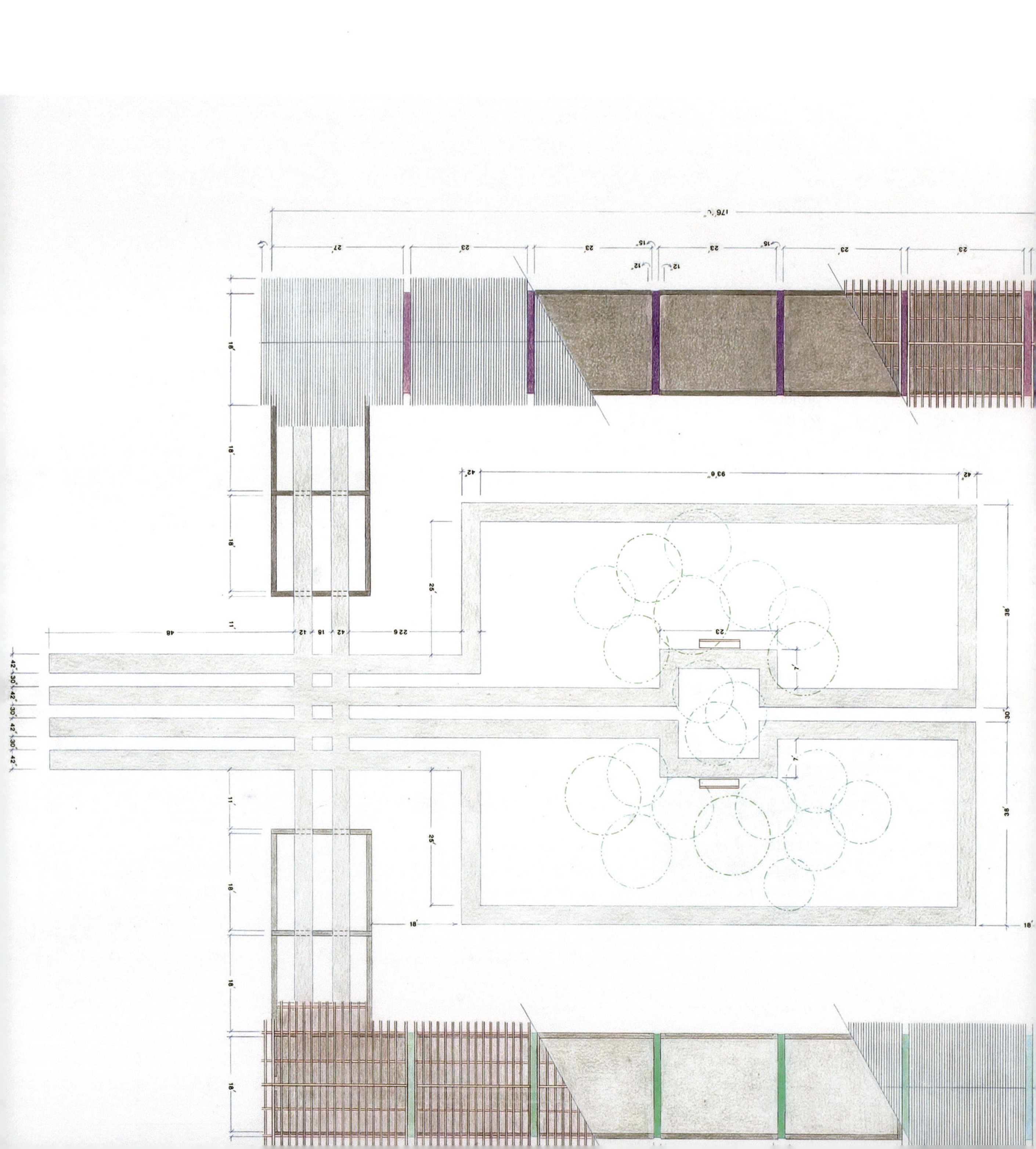

Introduction by
Matthew Simms

Robert Irwin: Site Determined explores four decades of the artist's outdoor environmental projects through his drawings and architectural models. Starting with Irwin's 1975 drawing for *Window Wall*, his first outdoor sculpture, the exhibition traces the gradually widening scope of Irwin's art through such ambitious projects as his *Arts Enrichment Master Plan* for the Miami International Airport and his *Central Garden* at the Getty Center. The exhibition culminates with a large group of drawings and two architectural models for *Untitled (dawn to dusk)*, one of Irwin's most important works to date, at the Chinati Foundation in Marfa, Texas.

Frequently associated with the Light and Space movement, Irwin got his start as an abstract painter in 1950s Los Angeles. Soon after, he began to question the conventions of painting, including its framing devices and representational assumptions. Irwin eventually "broke the frame,"[1] turning to the ambient environment itself as his medium. In the early 1970s, he made a series of subtle and elusive interventions in art galleries and museums with very simple materials, including scrim, string, and tape. Then, in 1975, Irwin took a crucial step outside, engaging directly with the outdoor world, moving beyond the traditional spaces of the art world and into the lived environment.

Irwin's site-determined art is less familiar than his better-known paintings and installations from the 1960s and early 1970s.[2] Nevertheless, Irwin himself has underscored the fact that his site-responsive work represents the culmination and realization of the aesthetic concerns he explored in more restricted ways in his earlier work.[3] This exhibition invites the visitor to witness the originality and breadth of Irwin's thinking as he develops unique responses to a range of outdoor and indoor/outdoor sites.

• • •

Organized chronologically, it begins with drawings for various projects on university campuses, dating from 1975 to 1982, and a three-dimensional model from 1978. Moving into the mid-1980s, Irwin became involved in larger projects, resulting in, among other proposals, a design for the public spaces in Lower Manhattan's Battery Park City.

In 1986, Irwin was invited to join a conversation concerning the place of public art in the Miami International Airport. The result was his most ambitious proposal so far: to transform the entire airport site into a sequence of aesthetic and practical spaces contextually informed by the local South Florida environment. Irwin's drawings for the project lead the viewer through the stages of his thinking, from the macro level of the airport itself to the micro level of specific interstitial garden spaces.

Following on the heels of this project, Irwin was engaged to develop the *Central Garden* at the Getty Center, to which he applied the lessons of his ultimately unrealized Miami plan. The viewer can trace the development of Irwin's monumental, "modern" garden, as he termed it, through drawings and a three-dimensional model. Additional drawings and models for later projects—both realized and unrealized—in Chicago and Los Angeles, dating from 1990 to 2011, provide glimpses into Irwin's ever-expanding practice of site-determined art.

The final section of the exhibition focuses on Irwin's most recent project, at the former Fort D.A. Russell hospital building on the campus of the Chinati Foundation in Marfa, Texas. In its ruined state, with no roof or window panes, the building offered Irwin striking opportunities to create a visual dialogue between indoor and outdoor spaces. As witnessed in the drawings and architectural models, his response begins as a play with differently colored glass roof panels but ultimately evolves into a vocabulary of complementary dark and light-gray corridors, bisected by long scrim panels to catch the sunlight entering through rhythmically spaced windows.

Each project takes as its starting point the conditions, as Irwin understands them, of the site he has been invited to consider. The process of discerning these conditions, he has explained, begins far from the site itself, in the broader regional context, then gradually moves inward through what he terms "concentric rings."[4] Site-determined art, Irwin writes, "draws all of its cues (reasons for being) from its surroundings. This requires the process to begin with an intimate, hands-on reading of the site." "A quiet distillation of all of this," he adds, "determines all the facets of the 'sculptural response.'"[5]

Granted, Irwin's understanding of these conditions, and his decisions about how best to respond to them, were always highly subjective. Other observers, for instance, might have identified very different conditions than those emphasized by Irwin as most significant to any given site. That Irwin's site-determined responses are subjective is, moreover, fundamental to his approach, since the broader motivation of his art is precisely to underscore the value and importance of individual sensory experience.

Consequently, he calls upon the observer to respond in kind as a perceptive, subjective individual: "Does this 'piece,' 'situation,' or 'space,' make sense?" "Is it more interesting, more beautiful?" "How do I feel about it?" "And what does it mean to me?"[6] Site-determined art, Irwin declares, "seeks to discover and value the potential for experiencing beauty in everything."[7] Irwin's optimism within his work is infectious, and his invitation to set aside shared cultural and historical meanings in order to perceive—as if doing so for the first time— has never been more relevant. In a world saturated with mediated experience, recovering the value of first-hand perception becomes an urgent task.

• • •

In addition to tracing the development of Irwin's site-determined approach to art-making from 1975 to the present day, this exhibition also follows the simultaneous evolution of Irwin's practice as a draughtsman. Irwin's earliest drawing in this exhibition is a minimal, matter-of-fact construction document, reflecting the elementary nature of the white plasterboard piece it describes. Gradually, as color emerges as a critical element of Irwin's site-determined art, his drawings also become more elaborate and vibrant. This evolution reaches a crescendo with an early set of Marfa drawings, rich in orange and violet hues. In his final conception, however, Irwin embraces a monochromatic vocabulary that recalls from afar the elegant simplicity of the drawing that stands at the outset of the exhibition.

From his early work in graphite and pen on modest, opaque sheets of white paper to later work in colored pencil and transfer lettering on large, semi-transparent sheets of Mylar, Irwin's drawings fall into a range of formats, including the three architectural standards of ground plan, section, and front elevation. Some of his most striking drawings in this exhibition are rendered in axonometric projection, while still others are close-ups or details made either for comparison or for building specifications. In addition to drawings, there are three-dimensional models, the first built in 1978 in the context of Irwin's project for Ohio State University, and the most recent built in 2015 for his Chinati project. Finally, there are also photo-grids, which Irwin produced to support his presentations of the Miami International Airport redesign.

It should be noted that the drawings, models, and photographs in this exhibition were never intended by Irwin to be treated as art. They were functional, communicative tools generated to support the often lengthy and multi-staged processes of presentation, discussion, and response. In this sense, they point in the opposite direction of his actual, site-determined work. Seeking to establish shared reference points for decision making, these tools are, above all else, informational in focus and, therefore, geared toward establishing general consensus. Irwin's site-determined art, conversely, invites the observer to engage not with shared meanings but rather with her or his own individual, private sensations.

The works featured in this exhibition were designed to be part of a broad conversation about logistics, feasibility, and desirability—the sharing and comparing of opinions. These conversations are, of course, the flip side of the resulting art itself, which is resolutely oriented toward cultivating the singularity and freedom of individual experience at each site. And yet this individual address is possible only once consensus has been achieved, a project has been approved, and building instructions have been communicated. There is no site-determined art, in other words, without such preliminary drawings and communicative tools. They present a history of reflection and revision played out across Mylar pages, wooden models, and grouped photographs. Such behind-the-scenes expository documentation usually never makes it out of the artist's studio or the conference room. This exhibition aims to present these pieces as valuable in themselves, without denying or overlooking the difference between the documentation, on one hand, and the work they were developed to illustrate and explain, on the other.[8]

The exhibition catalogue has been conceived as an opportunity to present new scholarship and perspectives, not only on Irwin's site projects but also on the drawings, models and conversations that prepared the ground for them. My essay, "From Light and Space to Site-Determined Art," explores Irwin's move outdoors as part of his larger ambition to expand individual aesthetic perception beyond the parameters of the museum or gallery, and into the realm of shared public spaces. Sally Yard's essay, "Site Determined: An Unfolding in Time," considers Irwin's grand projects from the late 1980s and early 1990s: the Miami International Airport *Arts Enrichment Master Plan* and the *Central Garden* at the Getty Center. And in "The Rest is All Sky: Irwin in Marfa," Ed Schad zeroes in on Irwin's site project for the Chinati Foundation, which was opened to the public in 2016.

• • •

After viewing the exhibition, visitors will be encouraged to take a five-minute walk from the museum to Irwin's newly conserved 1975 sculpture, *Window Wall,* on the California State University, Long Beach campus—supplementing their contemplation of Irwin's drawings, models, and photo-grids with a direct encounter with the artist's earliest site-determined outdoor sculpture. Visitors can further build upon their museum experience with visits to Irwin's other local, site-determined pieces, including *Palm Garden* at the Los Angeles County

Museum of Art, the *Central Garden* at the Getty Center, and *Sentinel Plaza* in Pasadena. In San Diego, visitors can see Irwin's *Two Running Violet V Forms*, part of the Stuart Collection on the campus of the University of California, San Diego, an early conceptual drawing for which appears in this exhibition. Also in San Diego, visitors can see *1°2°3°4°*, a site-determined piece at the Museum of Contemporary Art San Diego, as well as his Cor-Ten steel ramp at the San Diego Federal Court House. And finally, for those who can make the trip, a visit to Marfa, Texas is the logical next step, since this most recent site-determined piece is among Irwin's most significant and profound achievements in his nearly seven decades as an artist.

Notes

1   Robert Irwin, "The State of the Real: Robert Irwin Discusses the Activities of an Extended Consciousness," in *Notes Toward a Conditional Art*, ed. Matthew Simms (Los Angeles, CA: J. Paul Getty Museum, 2011), 53.
2   See, for example, Evelyn Hankins, et al., *Robert Irwin: All the Rules Will Change* (Washington, DC: Hirshhorn Museum and Sculpture Garden, 2016).
3   Irwin, interview with the author, April 2016, San Diego, CA.
4   Ibid.
5   Irwin, "Introduction," in *Being and Circumstance: Notes Toward a Conditional Art* (Larkspur Landing, CA: The Lapis Press, 1985), 27.
6   Ibid, 28.
7   Ibid, 29.
8   In exhibiting Irwin's drawings, models, and photographs we take our cue from Irwin himself, who first exhibited project documentation in 1985 in an exhibition at the Pace Gallery in New York. Irwin first exhibited project drawings in 1977 as part of a retrospective exhibition at the Whitney Museum of American Art in New York.

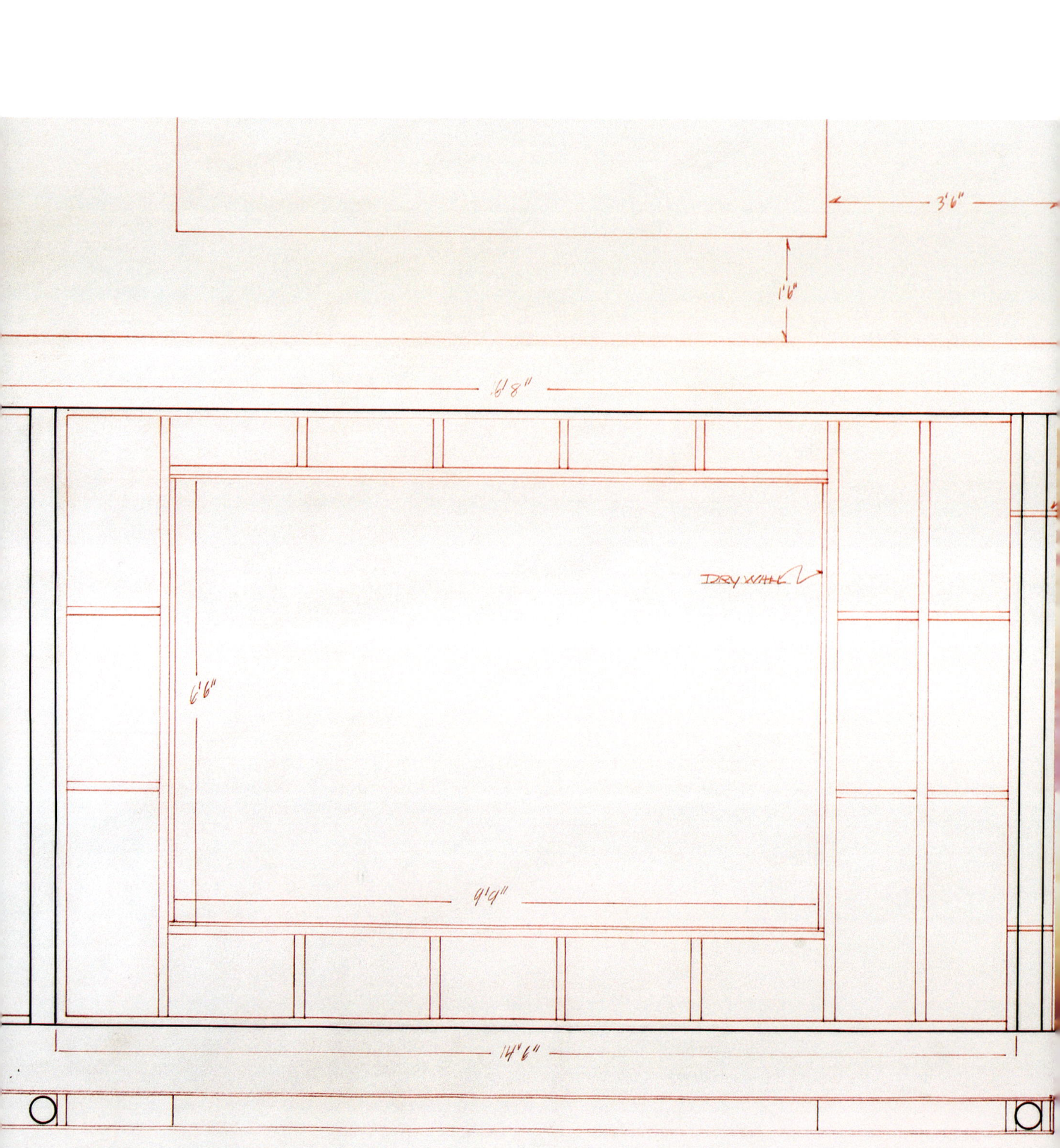

3'6"
1'6"
6'8"
DRY WALL
6'6"
9'9"
14'6"

FROM LIGHT AND SPACE TO SITE-DETERMINED ART

Matthew Simms

In a short review published in the October 18, 1975 issue of *Art Week*, critic Melinda Wortz draws her readers' attention to Robert Irwin's *Window Wall*, which had recently appeared on the campus of California State University, Long Beach. It was part of a small exhibition showcasing works by Southern Californian artists exploring issues of visibility and transparency, either through materials such as glass and acrylic resin, or by other means.[1] In keeping with his recent shift toward what he had begun to call, variously, site-responsive, site-conditioned, or site-determined art, Irwin chose to make an artwork that would interface directly with the conditions of the gallery's architectural context. "In the low keyed manner characteristic of his recent installation pieces," Wortz explains, Irwin "simply constructs a wide, rectangular frame within the space between two structural pillars." The piece, she continues, both confused and heightened perception:

> Some viewers perceive the unostentatious, white structure as part of the architecture rather than an ART piece. Actually, Irwin intends to make the art connotations of his work as nearly invisible as possible, using them only to alter minimally an already given space in order to sharpen the viewer's perceptual awareness. In this case the white frame serves to heighten both the color and the clarity of the landscape elements, and people moving within its boundaries.[2]

Perhaps thinking of the theme of the exhibition—*A View Through*—Irwin singled out the inherent focusing potential of the campus architecture, with various views and vistas formed into framed pictures through its repeated horizontal and vertical elements. By dropping a frame into a busy passageway between the art department and neighboring buildings, he invited the pedestrian moving through that space to stop and look through it, as if momentarily releasing the prospect from its practical context and allowing it to be contemplated as an exclusively aesthetic phenomenon. This single frame focuses attention in two directions: depending upon what side one stands, the viewer either gazes into the architectural space adjacent to the art gallery, or looks out from under the covered walkway toward the lawns, trees, and students in the quadrangle.

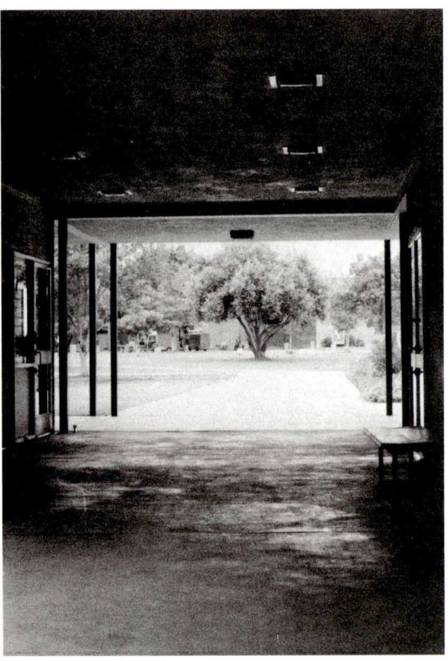

View of site selected by Robert Irwin for *Window Wall*, California State University, Long Beach, 1975.

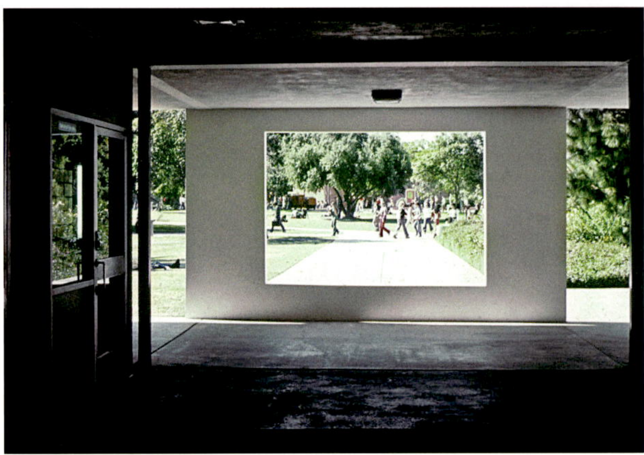

Robert Irwin, *Window Wall*, 1975. California State University, Long Beach. Wood, sheetrock, and white paint, 80 x 109 x 6 inches (203.2 x 276.9 x 15.3 cm). Collection of California State University, Long Beach.

Irwin wanted to deemphasize, as much as possible, what Wortz terms *Window Wall*'s "art connotations," blending it into its environment. The white, wall-like structure is visually continuous with its neighboring walls and the flat, white ceiling. Moreover, Irwin's elementary, black- and red-pen drawing, made to guide construction, reveals how he took advantage of existing architectural supports to build his window-like frame directly into the breezeway (plate 1).

None of this was new for Irwin. For over a decade, in fact, he had been exploring ways to break down the opposition between artwork and environment. Beginning in the early 1960s, he had become troubled by the rectangular framing edges of the canvas, which he increasingly regarded as placing arbitrary, conventional limits upon his paintings. As he puts it: "I sensed the world around me opening out, not closed in."[3] Seeking to "break the frame," he developed strategies to render ambiguous where the work of art ended and where its surrounding context began.[4] This led to Irwin's convex disc paintings, which merged, confusingly, with shadows projected on the wall behind them. He then extended this exploration to sculpture, with a series of transparent, cast acrylic columns. Fusing visually with the surrounding space, Irwin's columns gave away their locations only by means of the glints, reflections, and spatial distortions picked up by viewers moving around them.

Still not completely satisfied with these solutions, by 1970 Irwin had left painting and sculpture behind to work directly with architectural spaces, manipulating and channeling existing qualities of light, shadow, and volume. One of his preferred tools for doing so was scrim, a sheer nylon material that could look variously transparent or opaque, depending on how light fell upon it. He also employed wire, string, black tape, fluorescent light, and natural illumination. With "the simplest of means," as one contemporary observer noted, Irwin produced "powerfully space-altering effects."[5] In pieces in galleries and museums across the country, Irwin responded to the conditions of the indoor architectural spaces where he was invited to work. The distinction between art and its exhibition context became

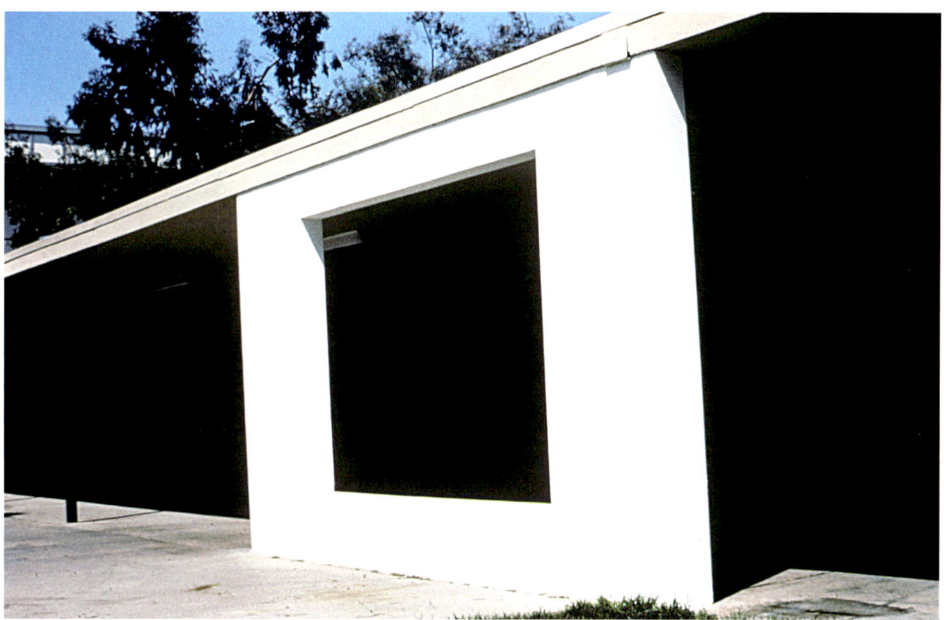

Robert Irwin, *Window Wall*, 1975. California State University, Long Beach. Wood, sheetrock, and white paint, 80 x 109 x 6 inches (203.2 x 276.9 x 15.3 cm). Collection of California State University, Long Beach.

especially untenable in these environmental installations, in which conditions of light, volume, space, and time were the elements of Irwin's work itself.[6]

With *Window Wall*, Irwin extended these activities to the outside world and engaged directly with the ambient, exterior environment. Wortz confirms the novelty of the piece: "The work differs from other Irwin installations I have seen in its use of an outdoor setting which is full of movement rather than empty, interior space."[7] The frame, or rectangular edge, which Irwin had found so arbitrary as a painter, now became an effective way to call attention to otherwise overlooked, background phenomena. Irwin made a minimal intervention into an existing architectural context as a way to interrupt habitual traffic flows, forcing the pedestrian either to walk around it or to look through it. *Window Wall* frames the ambient light, shadow, color, and activity out in the quadrangle, or, conversely, under the covered breezeway, underscoring what is usually ignored as meaningless background noise, and elevating it to something aesthetically significant in its own right. Irwin's ambition was to turn attention back on the spectator, asking her or him to extend aesthetic attention beyond the confines of the art gallery to the phenomena captured in *Window Wall*'s double gaze: raking light falling across a walkway, spots of colorful clothing against an emerald-green lawn, reflected light splashing onto the breezeway ceiling, etc. *Window Wall* is an invitation to the passerby to tarry in the here and now of aesthetic contemplation—"perceiving yourself perceiving," in Irwin's words.[8] "If you take that with you," he explains, referring to the heightened aesthetic attention he hoped to engender with such a gesture, "you will begin to see things everywhere around you." It's not the world that has changed, Irwin insists: "you are the one that is changed."[9]

$\bullet \ \bullet \ \bullet$

Window Wall was a temporary installation whose presence made sense in relation to the concurrent campus exhibition. It was site-determined, not only in its response to the CSULB

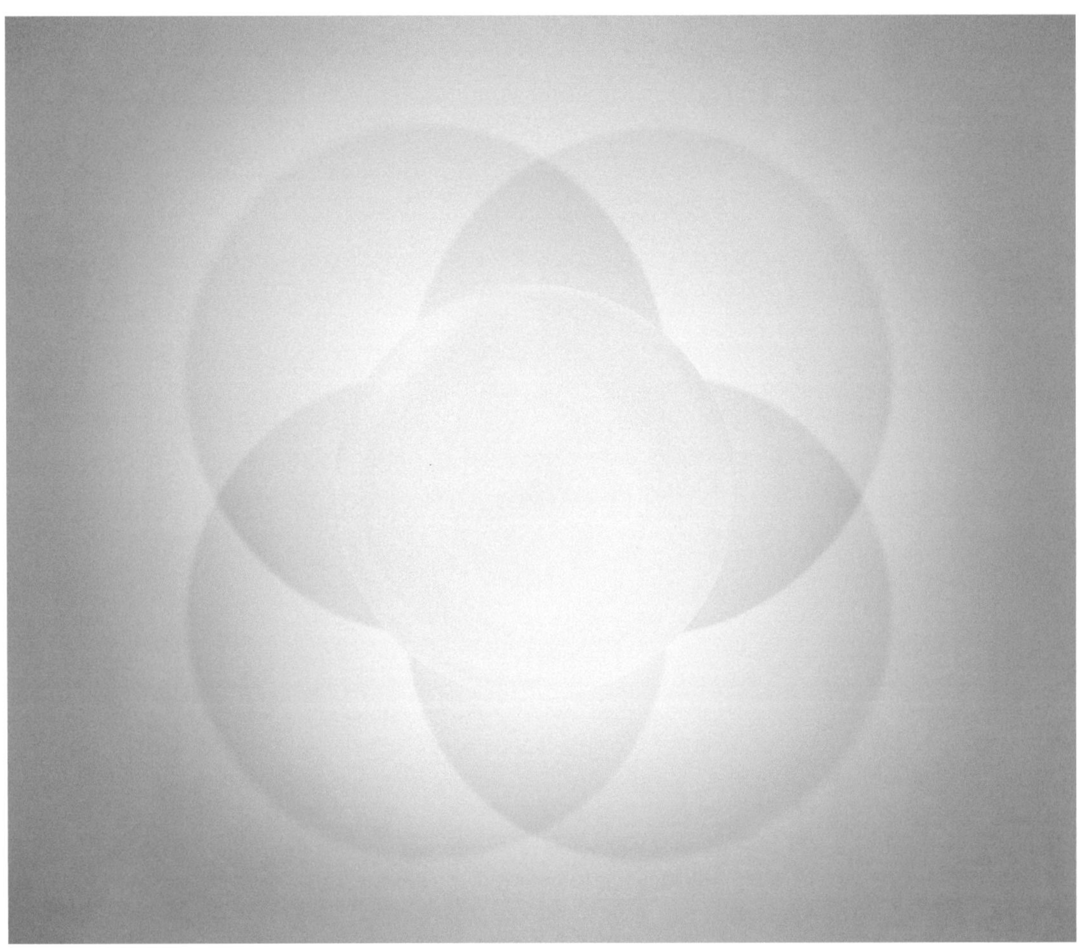

Robert Irwin, *Untitled*, 1966–7. Acrylic lacquers on shaped aluminum disc, metal tube, and four 150 watt lamps, 60 x 60 x 3 1/2 inches (152.4 x 152.4 x 8.9 cm). Hirshhorn Museum and Sculpture Garden, Smithsonian Institution, Washington, DC. Joseph H. Hirshhorn Purchase Fund, 2007. The Panza Collection.

campus architecture, but also in its relationship with *A View Through*'s investigation around issues of visibility and transparency.[10] Later, in 1978, Irwin began to accept invitations to propose permanent installations in a wide range of contexts, from more university campuses to city squares and public parks. These pieces no longer were linked to exhibitions, but now were conceived and pitched as stand-alone, outdoor works of art.

Tilted Planes, proposed for the Oval Mall at Ohio State University in Columbus, represents the beginning of Irwin's expansion into art in public places. Irwin first detailed his approach to the Sculptural Advisory Committee. "It is my particular process," he writes, "to develop an intimate solution so that anyone actively participating can directly reference the appropriateness of the sculpture to the particular set of circumstances," to which he adds that no special knowledge is required—anyone can "enjoy the event of the sculpture."[11] Irwin's "intimate solution" began with a general exploration of the campus, including architecture and landscape features, as well as patterns of traffic and use. He was struck by the Oval Mall's informal geometry of crisscrossing paths, which became alternately busy or quiet, depending on class schedules. Irwin also detected a slight concavity to the mall: "Because of the scale and the ever-so-slight 'bowl,' of the Oval, the different sections of grass, triangles, etc., take on the optical illusion of rising and tilting."[12] Irwin's proposal was meant

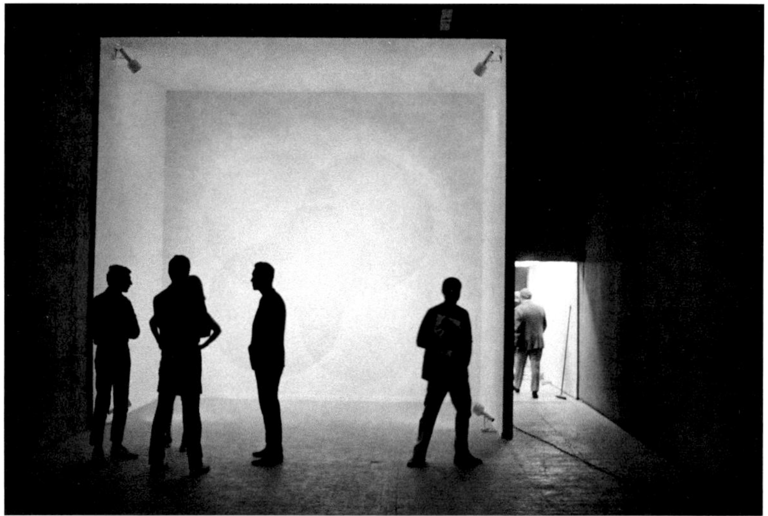

Installation view of Robert Irwin, *Untitled*, 1966–7, Documenta 4, Kassel, Germany, 1968.
Getty Research Institute, Los Angeles (2011.M.30), Special Collections, Harald Szeemann
papers, 2952-268, box 142.

to "activate" this effect, which was already, if only subliminally, present at the site. He would
tilt in various directions some, but not all, of the grass planes created by the intersecting
paths, shoring up the elevated sides with Cor-Ten steel retaining walls. "The planes would
just be tilted very slightly," Irwin explains in the proposal: "Zero to 18 inches might happen
over 100 feet."[13] Irwin's presentation drawing and three-dimensional model render the
overall conception. (He notes in his proposal that the planes "had been increased slightly in
the model for clarity") (plates 2 and 3).

"This, it seemed to me," Irwin recalls, "would have been the perfectly integrated figure/
ground sculpture."[14] Perfectly integrated, but not so integrated as to lose awareness that
changes to the landscape had taken place: "It was integrated and yet active."[15] Irwin's project
won the competition, but it was never realized, in part because of the success with which it
masked its status as art. "The Dean's question, 'Where's the sculpture?,' " Irwin notes, wryly,
"proves my point."[16]

The artist had better luck in 1981, when he was invited by the Stuart Collection to propose
an ambitious outdoor sculpture on the campus of the University of California, San Diego. He
again sought an "intimate solution" based on his individual response to the character of the
spaces on campus, including their use patterns. As Mary Beebe, the director of the Stuart
Collection, recalls: Irwin "responded particularly to the many eucalyptus groves scattered
around ... [t]hey are a dominant feature of the UCSD campus, giving it a sense of place
unique among the ten University of California campuses."[17] Irwin settled on one specific
eucalyptus grove through which a path—a major thoroughfare for students, faculty, and
staff—led from the student center to the upper reaches of the campus. His proposal, *Two
Running Violet V Forms*, consisted of two long bands, one 48 feet and the other 120 feet in
length, of plastic-coated, blue-violet, small-gauge chain-link fencing. The fifteen-foot-wide
bands, arranged in folded V shapes, would be held aloft in the eucalyptus canopy by tall
stainless-steel poles, high above the heads of pedestrians. From the perspective of the path,
the poles partially blend in with the eucalyptus trunks, which were planted at roughly eight-
foot intervals; while the bands of blue-violet fencing seem to pull the color of the sky down
into the foliage of the trees.

Robert Irwin, *Room Angle Light Volume*, 1971. Ace Gallery, Los Angeles. Synthetic fabric, wooden runner, fluorescent lights, and floodlights, 420 1/10 x 420 1/10 x 204 3/10 inches (1067 x 1067 x 519 cm).

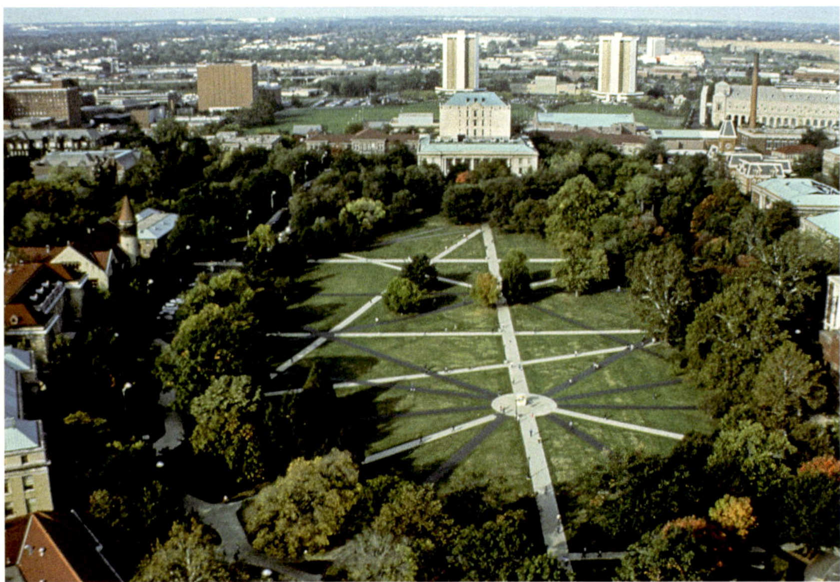

View of proposed site for Robert Irwin, *Tilted Planes*, Oval Mall, Ohio State University, Columbus, Ohio.

"I did some research," Irwin recalls, "looking for something that had the ability to affect a lot of space but was not something you focused on, was not a thing in itself, and that fence material from a little bit of a distance becomes just a visual haze of color." "The color is quite quixotic," he adds: "Sometimes the color is intense, really strong, and then sometimes it's not there at all."[18] The piece offered the opportunity for what Irwin terms a "natural confrontation." "Not art per se," he continues, "but perceptual interaction with 'phenomena' unattended or overly habituated—an art that calls us to attend to the pure potential in our circumstances as a whole piece."[19]

Irwin's early conceptual drawings for this project depict just one, six-panel V form, which corresponds to neither of the two final forms, both of which consist of eight panels in different configurations. In the most developed drawing, the sequences of parallel red pen lines running in opposite directions stand in for the warp and weft of the fencing itself and hint at the moiré effect created when two areas of fencing overlap (plate 4). Shorter green and red dashes lower on the page indicate Irwin's initial thoughts about ground cover, which became in the final piece a bedding of violet and green ice plants. The drawing is in axonometric projection, rather than geometric perspective, which Irwin generally eschews. Irwin's avoidance of perspectival drawings and his preference for what can be termed the "de-anthropomorphized" spaces of parallel projection, plans, and front elevations, allows him to jealously protect the uniqueness of the individual observer's situated experience.[20] Consequently, Irwin's drawings refer to conceptual structure and not to aesthetic perception. They present site-determined projects in the vocabulary of synthetic, mental images rather than in terms of what they eventually are destined to become: subjective events unfolding in the divergent experiences of individual, empirical observers.

Avoiding perspective drawings, ultimately, meant refusing to predict individual experience, a gesture that recalls Irwin's unwillingness, in the 1960s, to allow photographs of his paintings to appear in art magazines or catalogues. Doing so, he objected, robbed the viewer of the very thing that mattered most—the opportunity to encounter the work of art directly and without pre-interpretation or prejudice.[21] By extension, Irwin's refusal of the format of perspective drawing avoids "previewing" the individual experience of the observer in the context of his site-determined projects. In Irwin's San Diego drawings, consequently, the movement of the panel away from the viewer in space is not accompanied by a corresponding diminution in scale; that is, there is no recession of orthogonals toward a putative vanishing point. No vanishing point means no vantage point and, consequently, no mimicking of an observer's viewpoint.[22]

• • •

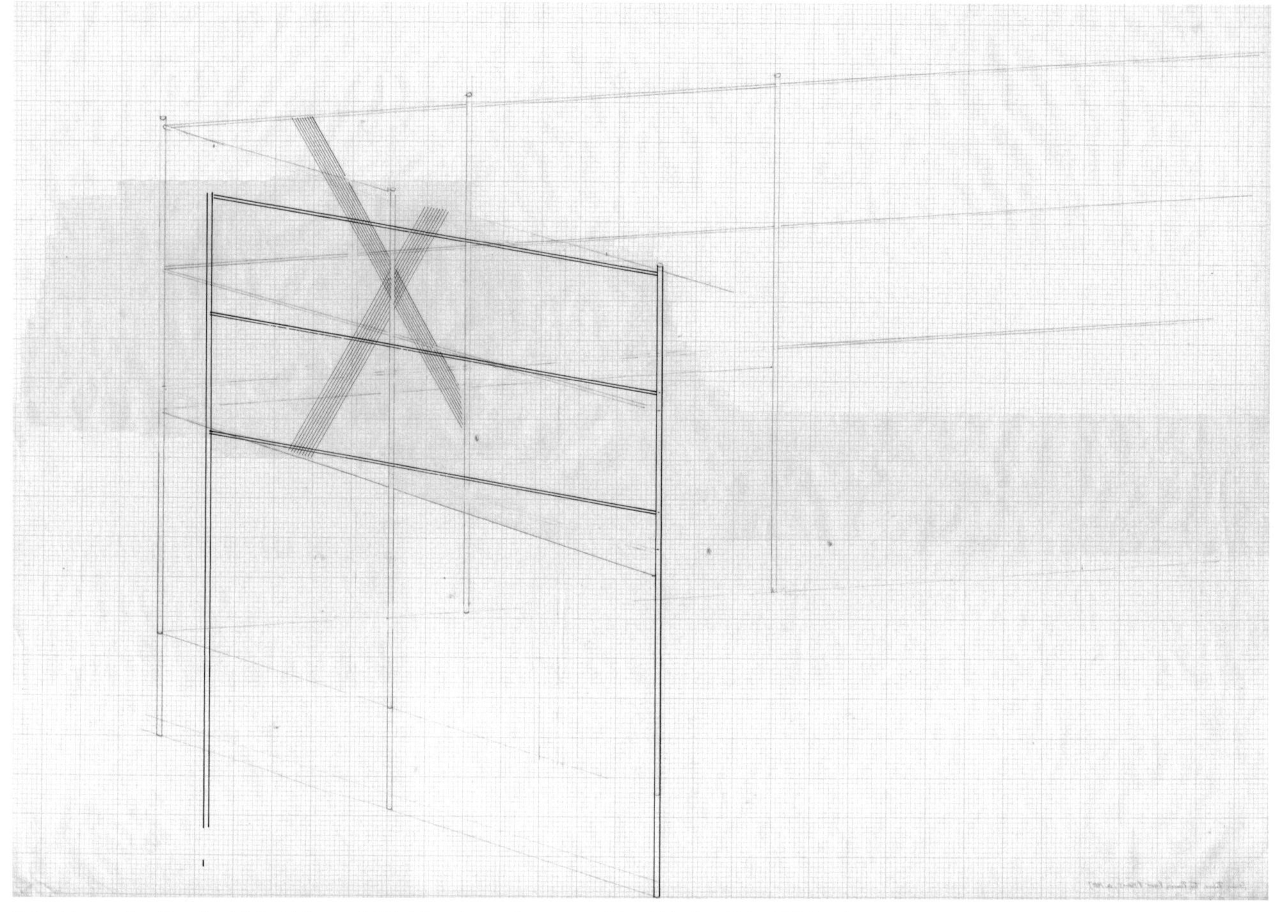

Robert Irwin, *Two Running Violet V Forms*, 1982. Ink and pencil on paper, 24 x 46 inches (61 x 116.8 cm).
Stuart Collection Records, Special Collections & Archives, University of California, San Diego.

As can be seen in the three projects discussed so far—*Window Wall*, *Tilted Planes*, and *Two Running Violet V Forms*—Irwin's commitment to working in a site-determined manner demanded flexibility with regard to materials and techniques. "I'll use any materials," Irwin declares, "any techniques (I don't care if somebody else is using them or seems to have them earmarked; I don't care if they're thought of as nonart), *anything that references against the specific conditions of the site*. Whether it works or not is my only criterion."[23] Irwin's use of white plaster in Long Beach was keyed to the existing architecture, whereas his turn to sod and Cor-Ten steel in Columbus was based on the existing grass and earthen hues of the site. In San Diego, Irwin used blue-violet, chain-link fencing and stainless-steel poles, a decision that was determined by his desire to have the piece blend in with the stand of trees while seeming to trap the sky within the eucalyptus canopy.

In still other contemporary projects, Irwin employed a diversity of materials, including granite rock, glass planes, flowering plants, deciduous and evergreen trees, and even exotic birds. When Irwin was invited to propose a piece for a defunct park in New Orleans, he came up with a plan for a massive aviary that would reference not only local flora and fauna, but also the Audubon Zoo, which was located in a distant corner of the city.[24]

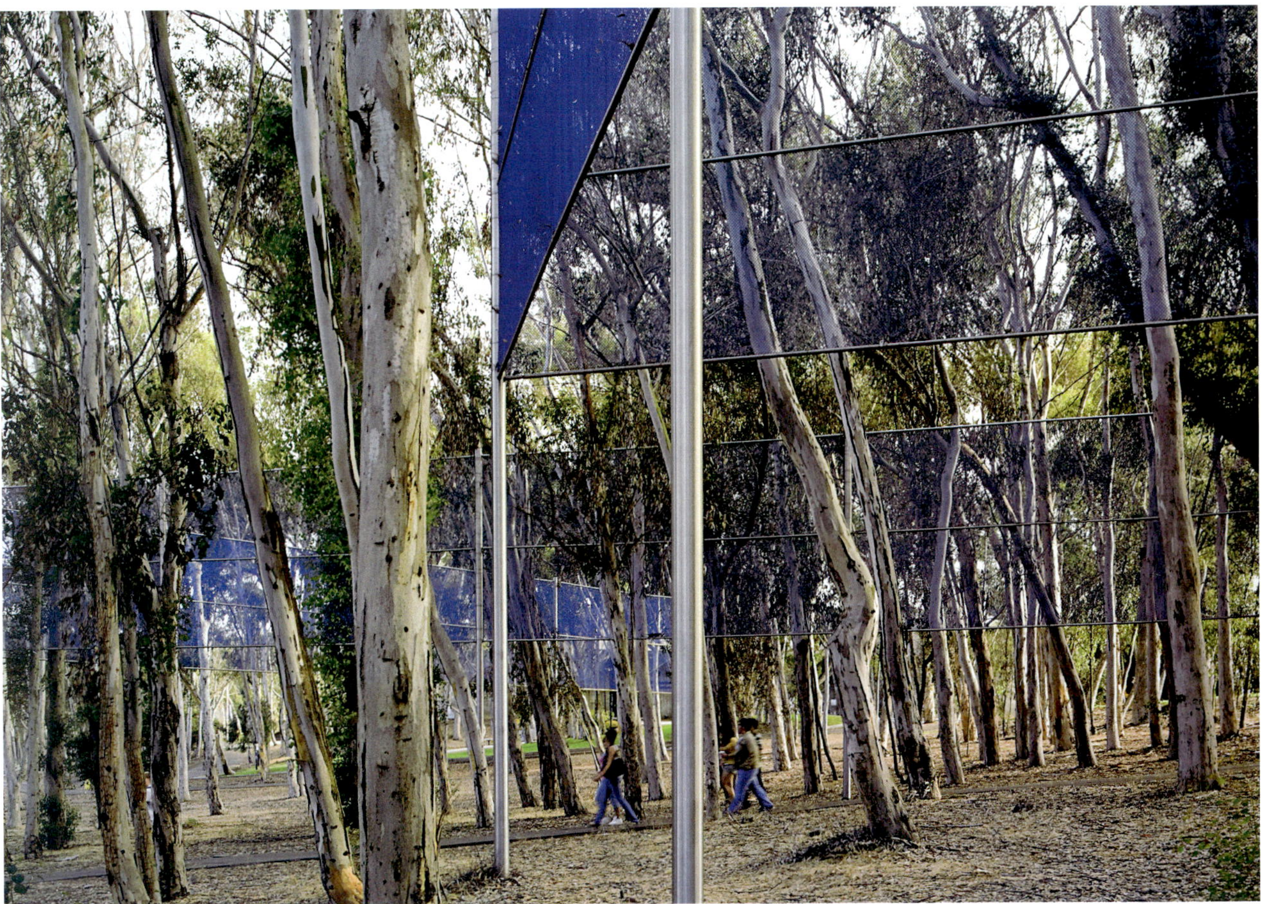

Robert Irwin, *Two Running Violet V Forms*, 1983. University of California, San Diego. Stainless steel poles and cross members, plastic-coated 5/8 inch (1.6 cm) aperture fencing, stainless steel fittings and turnbuckles, and ice plant. Two V-shaped forms each: 336 x 2352 inches (853.4 x 5974.1 cm); pole diameter: 5 inches (12.7 cm). Stuart Foundation Sculpture Collection, University of California, San Diego.

In each case, Irwin made his decisions based on the conditions of the site as he perceived and understood them. This does not mean, however, that he would not, on occasion, gravitate toward apparently analogous solutions. For example, he opted for long steel walls to create perceptual figure/ground play in two geographically distant projects, the first in Dallas, Texas, titled *Portal Park Slice*, and the second in Wellesley, Massachusetts, titled *Filigreed Steel Line*. The former consists of a tall, knife-like, Cor-Ten blade cutting dramatically through a park and busy intersection on Dallas' north side. The latter is a low, stainless-steel wall with plasma-cut, leaf-like patterns offering glimpses of a distant lake through its burnished surface. Irwin also occasionally availed himself of one and the same material for two or more different interventions. This is true, for example, of his recourse to Cor-Ten steel both for *Tilted Planes* and for *Portal Park Slice*. Likewise, he also used wide panels of blue-violet, chain-link fencing, such as the one in *Two Running Violet V Forms*, for a roughly contemporary project in Seattle, titled *9 Spaces, 9 Trees*. In each case, however, materials were chosen according to Irwin's sense of the conditions at each site and, once employed, took on a highly specific resonance and effect in this unique, singular context.[25]

All of this ultimately set Irwin far apart from other artists who made outdoor, public sculpture. "Traditionally," Irwin explains, "the art object was thought to be 'site-dominant.' "

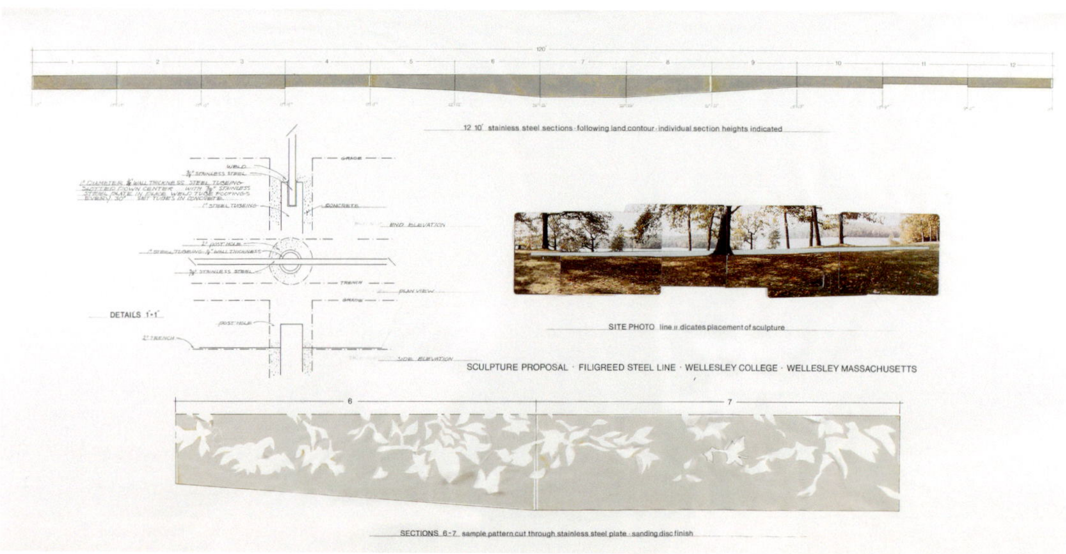

Robert Irwin, *Sculpture Proposal: Filigreed Steel Line, Wellesley College*, 1980.
Graphite, pen and ink, collage, acetate Letraset, and color photographs, 24 x 48 inches (61 x 121.9 cm).
Davis Museum at Wellesley College, Wellesley, Massachusetts, Gift of the Artist, 1980.28

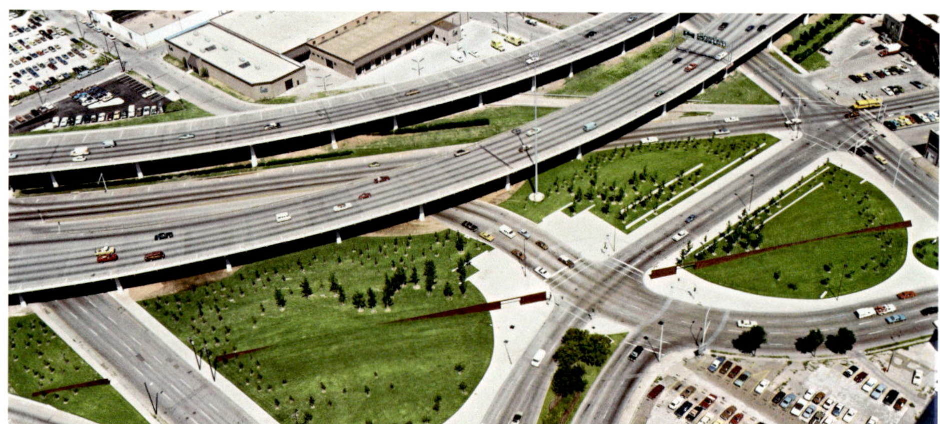

Robert Irwin, *Portal Park Slice*, 1978. Carpenter Plaza, Dallas, Texas. Cor-Ten steel, concrete footings, and earthen mounds (grass). Steel wall: 0 to 144 x 8400 x 1 inches (0 to 365.8 x 21336 x 2.5 cm).

It could be transplanted anywhere: in its transcendent significance it would dominate any location of placement. A recent representative of that tradition would be someone like Henry Moore. During the sixties, many artists began to think in terms of "site-adjusted" works. Mark Di Suvero, for example, will vary the scale and adjust the direction of placement (the compass coordinates) depending on the particulars of the site where he is placing one of his large pieces. By the seventies, people like Bob Morris were beginning to talk about "site-specific" art: that is, they would visit a site and tailor their proposal to the particular character of the site; but it was still very much their ideas overlaid onto this particular new site.[26]

Site-determined art, Irwin continues, represents the fourth and last site-oriented stage in this sequence. "The site in its absolute particularity," Irwin explains, "dictates to me the possibility of response."[27] Even "site-specific" sculpture tends to favor stylistic consistency over sensitivity to a site. Irwin's site-determined art, conversely, is self-consciously eclectic in style and materials, replacing the recognizable authorial gesture with responsiveness to the inherent conditions of the site. "What I am saying," Irwin explains, "is, if I did it properly ... if I did something in a particular set of circumstances that was perfectly resonant with those circumstances, then as you come along you don't have to know anything about me, and you don't have to know anything about art.

"You have all the same clues that I had," he underscores, "you have all the same references that I had, and you can essentially go through the same immediate processing." In the end, Irwin declares: "It's about perception, it's about awareness, it's about consciousness."[28]

• • •

In 1985, Irwin exhibited the results of a decade of site-determined work at the Pace Gallery in New York. The exhibition, which included drawings, photographs, and models, documented fourteen projects, of which eight had been realized, three were in limbo, and three had been scuttled. *New Yorker* art critic Calvin Tomkins reviewed the "puzzling" show, noting "the photographs and drawings, and even the scale models, of his projects gave so little sense of what it was like to experience them in situ."[29]

Of course, Tomkins admits, the documents were never meant to stand in for the work, but rather were intended to present information relating to Irwin's process of working toward specific solutions for a site. Among the projects documented in the exhibition was Irwin's ambitious proposal for the public spaces in and around Battery Park City, a three-and-a-half acre, commercial and residential, waterfront development on Lower Manhattan's west side. Irwin, along with a host of other artists, was invited to visit the site in early 1983. His impression of the site focused on three elements: the presence of the river, the awkward relationship of the harbor to the geometry of the rest of the site, and the "primary forms" of Cesar Pelli's architecture—the three towers he proposed to build around the North Cove plaza were capped with a dome, a pyramid, and a ziggurat, respectively.

Irwin sought to reference all three conditional elements—water, overlapping geometry, and elementary shapes. The shapes are the most immediate aspect of the plan: a sunken amphitheater in the form of an inverted dome; a raised bosque-like garden reached by the steps of a red-marble-stepped ziggurat; and a glass pyramidal conservatory thrust into the water, reached by a short pier. Irwin's elaborate color pencil drawing of the project, titled *Three Primary Forms*, reveals the overall conception and the repetition of circles, squares, and pyramid shapes, as do images of the model he presented to the committee (plate 5).

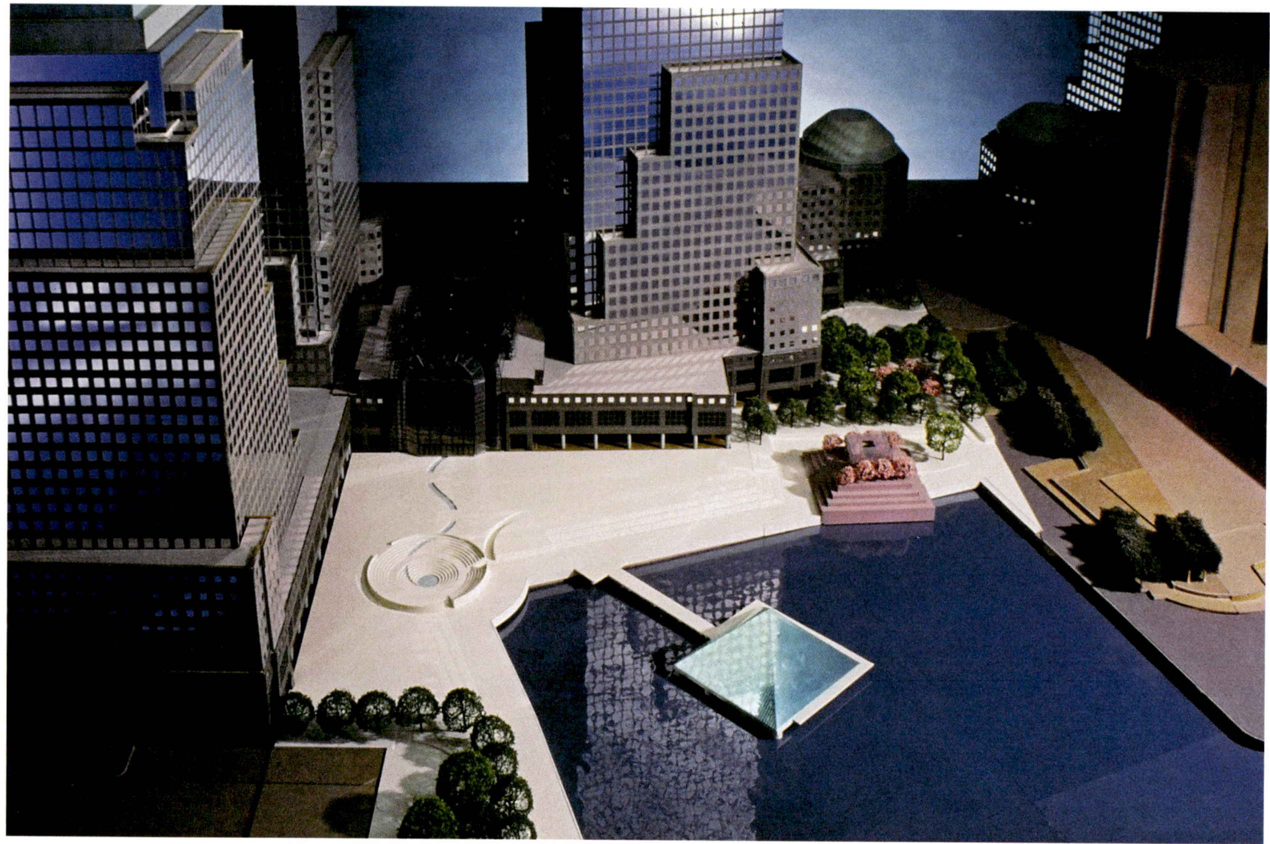

Robert Irwin, *Three Primary Forms (unrealized)*, 1983. Battery Park Commercial Plaza, New York, New York. Mixed media proposal model.

The drawing also shows the multiple axes of the site grafted upon one another: Irwin's plaza design aligns with the axis of the northern high-rise buildings, which are aligned with the existing city grid. His treatment of the harbor, however, allows it to cut through the space at an oblique angle, responding to the contour of the lower, tapering end of the island of Manhattan.[30]

And yet, the contrary geometry of the site was not meant to be grasped intellectually but rather was supposed to be felt as complex juxtapositions of now-aligning, now-diverging lines of sight and paths of ambulation. Irwin organized the plaza and esplanade in terms of ambulatory paths, moving into and out of the environment of the primary forms, and then through the more contemplative and less populous garden areas south of the lower tower. Describing the inverted dome, for example, he underscores how it "directs the flow of pedestrian traffic through the most critical corner of the plaza," adding that "the steps, ring paths, and curved ramps each articulate the foot traffic in a variety of ways."

The stepped pyramid was equally oriented to guide traffic into specific patterns: "Note its placement so as to bring the walking path 'inside' between the walls of the pyramid and the formal garden to the south, thereby creating a change of pace and a sense of entrance to the plaza."[31]

Finally, the relationship of the three primary forms to their sources on the tops of Pelli's

towers would be established at best by sited, partial, oblique comparisons from the plaza
floor to the skyline above. Or, accounting for the views from the towers themselves, these
comparisons might be made by looking back and forth between the plaza below and the
shapes on the building roofs, now seen less obliquely, but still only partially. What is present
all at once in the drawing and model, in other words, would be encountered in a partial and
conditional manner by the observer in context. The aesthetic experience of the individual
observer, not the sculptural forms themselves, remained, here as elsewhere, Irwin's main
concern.

"His method is to set up environmental situations that encourage the viewer to look about
him with the eye of an artist," Tomkins explains. "No finite work of art can compare in
importance with this individual act of perception.[32] "In a sense," continues the critic, "he
is echoing the point that Marcel Duchamp made nearly thirty years ago. Duchamp said that
the artist performed only one part of the creative act. The other part was up to the onlooker,
whose response to and interpretation of what the artist had done completed the creative
cycle."[33] In fact, "Irwin goes further than Duchamp," Tomkins admits. "Art, for Irwin ... is a
particularized kind or state of awareness."[34] And this awareness, which historically has been
reserved for the artist, now also becomes the prerogative of the observer.[35]

Irwin was not awarded the Battery Park City commission, which instead went to the team
of Siah Armajani and Scott Burton, whose proposal turned attention away from the spatial
tensions that interested Irwin toward other, more symbolic and utilitarian concerns—a
pier-like structure and a bridge, as well as seating-as-sculpture. Although his work was
not chosen, a clear link can be traced between Irwin's concerns in this large, ambitious
project and the comparatively more modest *Window Wall*, which inaugurated his move
outdoors. Both were based on conditionally specific interventions and both were meant to
blur the boundaries of the work of art and its context, integrating one into the next, but
without losing a sense that something had happened to enhance or change the site. Both
projects, likewise, were intended to address the viewer not as a member of a group (the
campus, the art department, the public, or any other constituency) but rather as a unique,
perceiving, judging individual. It is this passerby who makes sense of Irwin's gesture, who
assesses it, who extends and develops it in her or his own experience, or who abandons it
as unconvincing. Aesthetic judgment, Irwin reminds us, is ultimately a singular affair, for
which the security of shared agreements is finally unavailable.

The difference between the modest construction drawing for *Window Wall* and the more
elaborate, colorful plan drawing and model for Battery Park City underscores the increasing
ambition and scope of Irwin's site-determined art from one decade to the next. Irwin's
Battery Park City project also included a hint of things to come in the form of an elaborate

garden, located in an area south of Pelli's Tower B, which Irwin describes as "carefully adjusted for season, color, smell, scale, texture."

"It's curious to me that no other proposal even mentioned planting," Irwin notes, which represents "a serious opportunity that artists generally overlook." After all, he continues: "Don't these organic instances present a sculptural opportunity? It seems odd to me not to consider the presence of trees, flowers, grass, etc., and their textures, colors, smells, and sounds as aesthetic potentials."[36] These remarks are indeed prophetic, since in the years following the Battery Park City competition, plants, flowers, and other organic materials increasingly made up some of Irwin's most important and compelling site-determined solutions. The aesthetic potential of gardens would become overwhelmingly evident in the grand site-determined garden projects Irwin would develop in the mid-to-late 1980s and into the 1990s, including the *Arts Enrichment Master Plan* for the Miami International Airport and the *Central Garden* at the Getty Center.

Notes

1   Constance W. Glenn, *A View Through* (Long Beach, CA: University Art Gallery, 1975).

2   Melinda Wortz, "Ephemerae," *Art Week*, vol. 6, no. 35, October 18, 1975, 2–3.

3   Robert Irwin, "The State of the Real: Robert Irwin Discusses the Activities of an Extended Consciousness," in *Notes Toward a Conditional Art*, ed. Matthew Simms (Los Angeles, CA: J. Paul Getty Museum, 2011), 52.

4   Ibid, 53.

5   Jane Livingston, "Robert Irwin," in Maurice Tuchman and Jane Livingston, *11 Los Angeles Artists* (Los Angeles, CA: Los Angeles County Museum of Art, 1971), unpag.

6   For a discussion of Irwin's development from painting to environmental art, see Matthew Simms, *Robert Irwin: A Conditional Art* (New Haven, CT and London: Yale University Press, 2016).

7   Wortz, "Ephemerae," 2–3.

8   Irwin, "The State of the Real," 53.

9   Irwin, [no title], typed transcript of lecture [ca. 1971], Robert Irwin file, 11, Los Angeles County Museum of Art (quoted in Simms, *Robert Irwin: A Conditional Art*, 103).

10 With Irwin's consent, *Window Wall* was made permanent after the end of the run of
    the exhibition. "Response to the subliminal architectonic sculpture ... was so great that
    Irwin gave his permission for it to be reconstructed in permanent materials in 1976" (Jane
    Bledsoe, letter to Nancy Lobdell, February 14, 1980, Robert Irwin file, University Art
    Museum, California State University, Long Beach).

11 Irwin, "Ohio State Proposal," in *Notes Toward a Conditional Art*, 185.

12 Irwin, "Ohio State University," in *Being and Circumstance: Notes Toward a Conditional
    Art* (Larkspur Landing, CA: The Lapis Press, 1985), 43.

13 Irwin cited in Lawrence Weschler, *Seeing Is Forgetting the Name of the Thing One Sees.
    Expanded Edition* (Berkeley and Los Angeles, CA: University of California Press, 2008), 202.

14 Irwin, "Ohio State University," 43.

15 Irwin cited in Weschler, *Seeing Is Forgetting*, 202.

16 Irwin, "Ohio State University," 43.

17 Mary Livingston Beebe, "Robert Irwin," in *Landmarks: Sculpture Commissions for the
    Stuart Collection at the University of California San Diego*, ed. Mary Livingston Beebe (New
    York, NY: Rizzoli International Publications, Inc., 2001), 63.

18 Irwin, "Interview with Joan Simon," in *Landmarks*, 67.

19 Irwin, "San Diego: University of California," in *Being and Circumstance*, 77.

20 Dorothée Imbert, "Skewed Realities: The Garden and the Axonometric Drawing," in
    Representing Landscape Architecture, ed. Marc Treib (London and New York: Taylor &
    Francis, 2008), 132.

21 Simms, *Robert Irwin: A Conditional Art*, 66–68.

22 Yve-Alain Bois, "Metamorphosis of Axonometry," in *Daidalos*, vol. 1, no. 1, September 15,
    1981, 40–58.

23 Irwin cited in Weschler, *Seeing Is Forgetting*, 196–197.

24 Irwin, "New Orleans," in *Being and Circumstance*, 119–125.

25 Simms, *Robert Irwin: A Conditional Art*, 147–183.

26 Irwin cited in Weschler, *Seeing Is Forgetting*, 197–198.

27 Ibid, 198.

28 Irwin, "Interview with Joan Simon," 72–73.

29 Calvin Tomkins, "Knowing in Action," *New Yorker*, November 11, 1985, 147.

30 Irwin, "New York," in *Being and Circumstance*, 99–103.

31 Ibid, 102.

32 Tomkins, "Knowing in Action," 147.

33 Ibid, 148.

34 Ibid.

35 Ibid.

36 Irwin, "New York," 102.

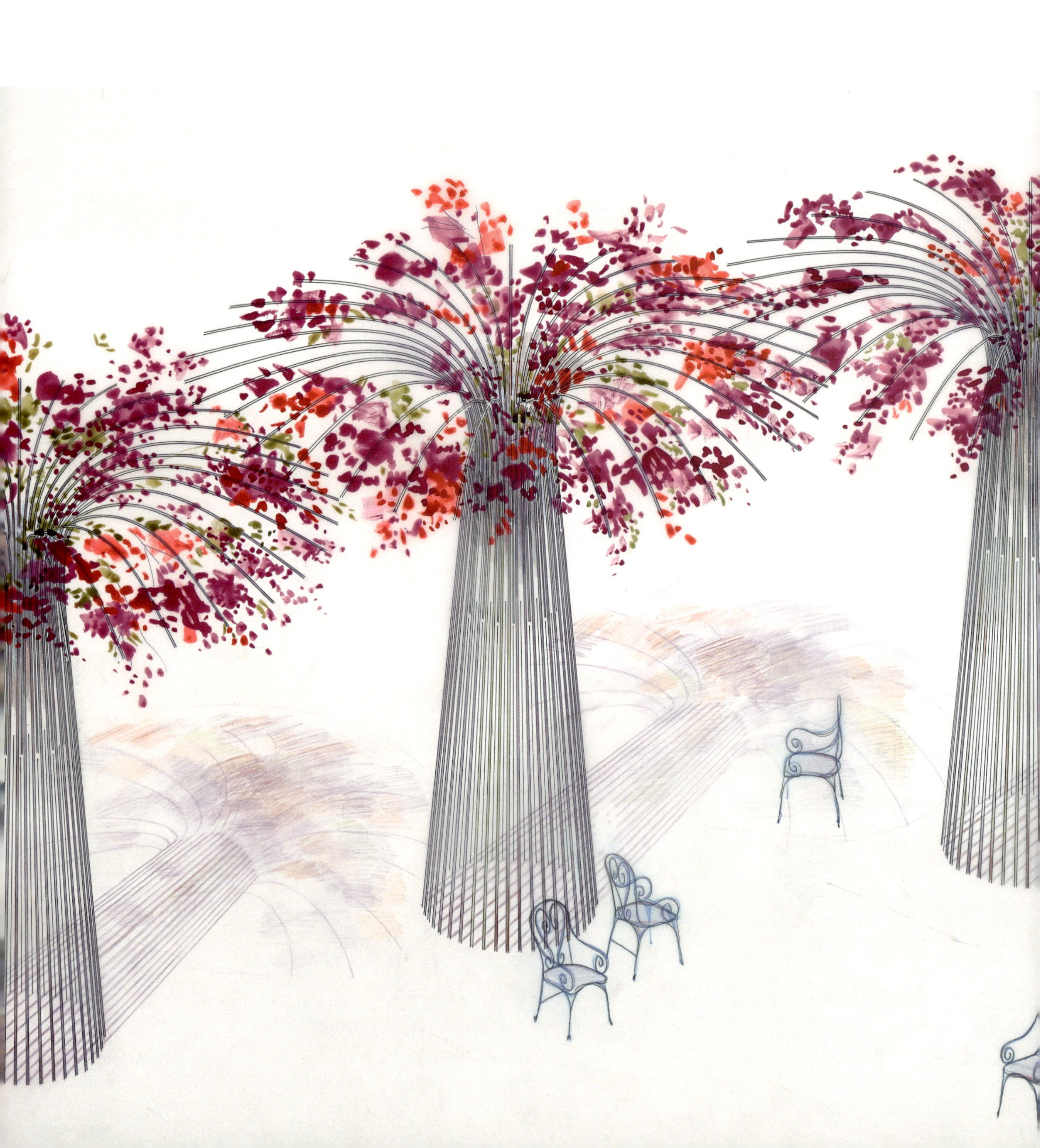

SITE DETERMINED: An Unfolding in Time

Sally Yard

Hurtling along the sun-baked straightaway of Central Boulevard toward the Miami International Airport, the traveler gradually enters the cool shade of a grove enveloping a gentle arc of road. A short distance ahead, the curve opens onto a causeway over a riverscape of reeds and sand spits, then pauses at a toll plaza. Mist rises from the marsh to the north, catching the sun or evening lights. From there, the route dips under a cool green canopy pierced by the electric-magenta of sun filtered through bougainvillea in the garden above. A pause, a place to park the car—a threshold into the airport. This, in any case, was the idea.

From the beginning, the parking garage—actually a shabby concrete structure worn down by South Florida humidity and unvented smog—was emblematic of the problems and possibilities of re-thinking the Miami International Airport. The oldest structures of the airport, as it stood in the mid-1980s, had been built in the 1950s, conceived to accommodate roughly 4,000,000 passengers each year and close to 100,000 tons of cargo. By the time Robert Irwin was invited to take a look at the unruly space in 1985, Miami International Airport had become the crucial transportation link between North and South America, circulating cargo and people around the clock. Greeting nearly 20,000,000 visitors each year and managing 1,000,000 tons of cargo, the airport's operations were centered in a single passenger terminal building and adjacent structures that had grown, over the quarter of a century, in response to immediate exigencies, with no overarching plan.

The timing of the invitation was felicitous for Irwin, who had already spent twenty years taking stock of art's potential to "weave the richness of our perceptions ... into the very fabric of our daily lives."[1] In temporary and permanent projects and in ardently reasoned writings, Irwin had put into action his notion of site-determined art. Moving away from the objects of art toward the "subject of art"—"the aesthetics of individual perception"[2]—Irwin had clarified for himself a trajectory he understood to have been set in motion by Kazimir Malevich's "desert of pure feeling" and Piet Mondrian's "culture of determined relations."[3] In identifying with such utopian modernists, he had staked out an ambition that was, he

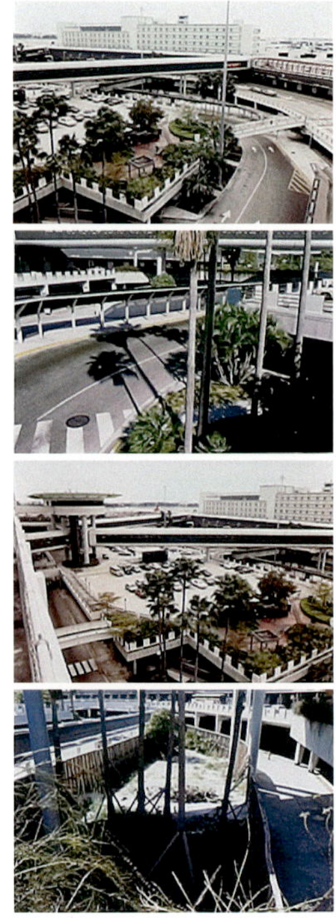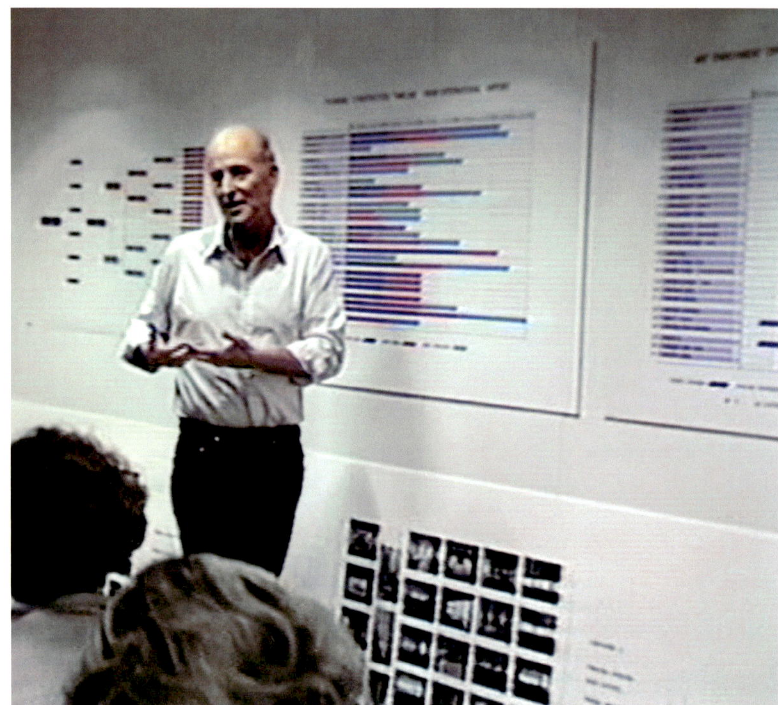

Left: Detail of *Arts Enrichment Master Plan, proposed 1986 (unrealized), Miami International Airport, Central Park, Second Presentation*, 1986 (Plate 13). **Right:** Robert Irwin presenting the Miami International Airport project to members of the Metro-Dade Art in Public Places Trust, September 23, 1987.

acknowledged, "probably not going to even get sorted out" in his lifetime.[4] And that was fine with him—given his sense of art's capacity to affect the world.[5]

The Miami airport project materialized as a chance to put to the test the ideas and questions Irwin had pondered in *Being and Circumstance: Notes Toward a Conditional Art* (published that year). Here was an opportunity to undertake a case study of how "we put in motion our values"[6]—a chance to examine motives and structures of decision making[7] at a momentous scale. The five-year process in Miami set the stage for Irwin's *Central Garden* at the Getty Center in Los Angeles. If the Miami plan was built around an experiential sequence that acknowledged the necessity of clarity and function, and forged the possibility of richness and reflection, then the Getty garden took up the charge of luring the visitor, slowly but surely, to attend to the enthralling character of the world—to focus on "this petal, that stalk."[8]

Four crucial realizations play out in the Miami airport project and the Getty *Central Garden*:
1. The possibilities are determined by the site.
2. The "infinite potential of human beings to see and to aesthetically order the world is the *one pure subject of art*."[9]
3. Perception unfolds over time, in the flux of things.[10]
4. There is "no better place" than a garden—"ever changing"—"to undertake an extended inquiry into the rhyme and reason for 'art in public places,' and ... to question the true nature of our being in the world."[11]

• • •

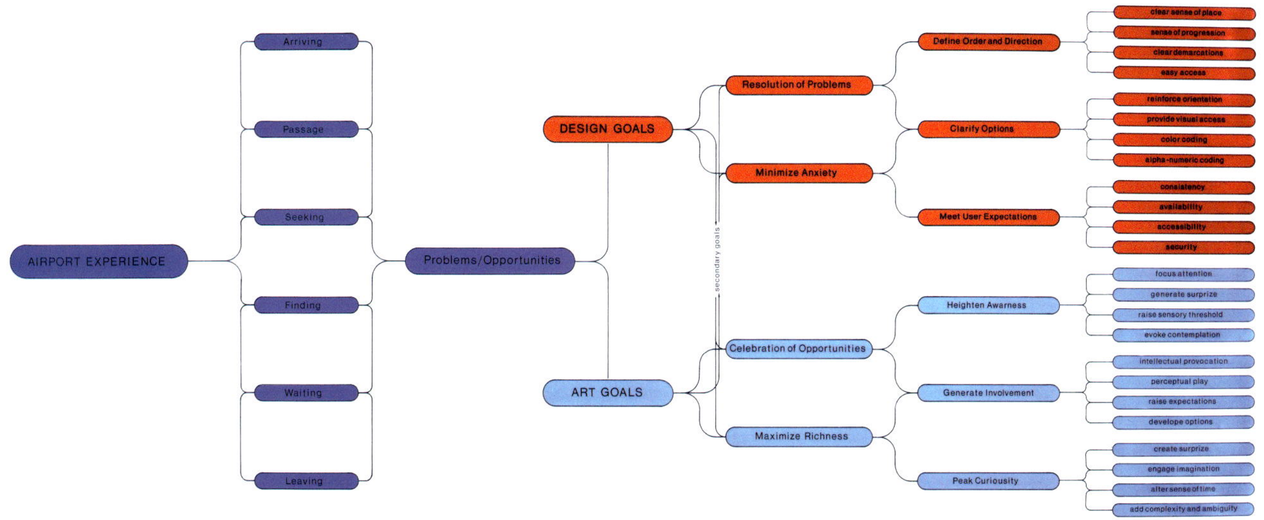

Robert Irwin, *Arts Enrichment Master Plan, proposed 1986 (unrealized), Miami International Airport, Airport Experience (First Presentation)*, 1986. Getty Research Institute, Los Angeles, Special Collections, Robert Irwin papers (940081), tube 26.

While the airport itself "could have been in Cleveland,"[12] Miami and surrounding South Florida were a luminous, tropical realm of broad, white-sand beaches; azure Atlantic waves; and tangled vegetation rising from humid swamplands a short distance inland. Irwin set to work to suggest the excitement of the place and the possibilities for "richness"[13] in an *Arts Enrichment Master Plan*, which would at once jumpstart the processes of artists invited to participate and jog the thinking of staff and consultants for the airport and Metro-Dade Art in Public Places. A "History of South Florida" stretched from the arrival of Ponce de Leon in 1513 (as legend has it, in pursuit of a fountain of youth), to the emergence in the 1980s of Miami as a "magic city" of "modern glassiness."[14] A "Mythology" ranged from real-estate boomers and "streamline modern" to *Miami Vice* and "Little Havana." Replete with a storied past and fantastical mythology, the city itself had burgeoned only after the "Mosquito War" of 1933 had made it habitable. From the "snowbird" vacationers escaping the winters of the northeast to successive waves of émigrés from Cuba, the population had grown quickly in numbers and complexity.[15]

A section of the *Master Plan* with the heading "Metaphor/Imaging" deploys descriptive words to evoke the qualities of "Tropical," "Topography: Land/Water Conditions," and "Light/Conditions." The passages are vivid, arranged in terms of "In Effect" (for example, "atmospheric diffusion [humidity] – fractured light – inter-reflections – dispersion – washed out shadows"); "In Experience" ("dancing light – mirages – shimmering seas"); and "In Response" ("refractive surfaces – absorbent surfaces – filtering surfaces—screens – grids – leaves").[16] A thorough "Project Listing" lays out the "Art Enrichment Opportunities," noting the principal strategies, primary methods, and proposed artists for each site. So, for instance, the principal strategies for the entrance drive gardens were: "define order & direction" and "heighten awareness." The primary methods were: "sense of progression, clear demarcation, focus attention, ceremonial-celebrative."[17]

SORCE FEATURES	EXPERIENCE	EFFECT iridescence	RESPONSE	compounded metaphor image metaphors
TROPICAL *(quixotic weather patterns)*	HOT-HUMID – thunder heads / WEATHER – HOT-HUMID / Torrential rains / Hurricanes – CORAL / at SOFT-AIR / warm (wet) evenings / complex skys	Bright colors in plants fish butterflies / vigorous growth / RAIN sounds · roof · falling water / saturated color – spots / exotic plant life / " Bugs " mosquitoes	Light clothing (casual) / strong use of color (Caribbean) / over grown gardens – roads / out door life – Tourism / Saturated / interior spaces (patios) / screened in porches / open architecture – closed air conditioned architect	retirement Tourism VACATION / free bldg to moving breeze / old → New →
LIGHT *(more complex skys)*	Brightness – white / glancing – HOT / High-skys – bounce / low-skys clouds / cloud Consciousness / lit at night / patterns on ground dark-light	Bleaching · pale / FADED COLORS – PASTELS / DARK-light-patterns / blending whites / sun exposure / shade Trees spreading / shadow · Dark green · black	ROADS white (bleached) / sun glasses · shades · hats / Tourism (sell sunshine) / Latin HUXlers / sunscreen / cool Dark interiors / shaded / NARROW ARCADES · covered walks · Arbors · overhangs	Arbors screening / Breezeways / ceramic roof tiles / Narrow (cool) arcades / tree lined streets / on bldgs
LAND *(f)*	OPEN – FLAT / Distance – infinity / High skys / HORIZON – LOST merge / Land-water-sky-merge / islands	Horizon – all around · merge with sky-water / (Land-water-sky-merge / Humid Light) / infinity distance / whites · warm / (Architecture Around / Turned away from street)	urban sprawl / no curbs / Long straight hywnys / Tall vertical palms / canals · waterways	
WATER	open water/land merge / interspaced with land / SEA BREEZE / CORAL	swamps – canals / High water Table – / GEs waterways / → cooling / AQUA-MARINE · Blue-green / surrounded by water	CAUSEWAYS · / Tilt up bridges / Build up off the ground / Boats – Sailing-speed / cruise ships / SEA planes connect all	life style elements / connect all nature elements plant life / connect all color elements / connect all architectural elements
AIR / compare with san Francisco / Hills / Historical events	SOFT – muggy	Historical forces / coral gables speculation / LAND / cuban revolution · Drugs / gateway · so · central America	NY (Jewish) winter migration / over development History in flux	

Robert Irwin, *Notes for Arts Enrichment Master Plan, proposed 1986 (unrealized), Miami International Airport*, 1986.
Getty Research Institute, Los Angeles, Special Collections, Robert Irwin papers (940081), box 23, file 9.

All of this would play out along the continuum that is "the nature of the airport experience"—"arrival – passage – seeking – finding – waiting – leaving"[18]—a sequence that would recur in successive iterations across the journey through the airport. Individual artists would take on each concourse, creating a "whole world,"[19] bringing on a team of other artists, designers, and fabricators. David Antin, Nam June Paik, and Joseph Kosuth envisioned projects for the baggage claim. Coy Howard took up the vertical access spaces within the "interstitial adjacencies"—those nodes where trajectories of passage converge.[20] Max Neuhaus, Charles Garabedian, Alice Aycock, Pablo Cano, John Baldessari, and Terry Allen were invited to think through one space or another. Taking its cues from Miami's stylized Art Deco architecture, Alexis Smith's plan for Concourse B incorporated a mural in which the continents of North and South America appear in a sea of clouds, pierced by a sculptural streamlined plane. Nearby, a sleek, circular bar of brass and chrome surrounds an illuminated globe against a backdrop of palm fronds etched in glass. Richard Fleischner envisioned an aviary and an aquarium invoking South Florida's wetlands and tropical ocean life, together with a sound work that would accompany travelers as they moved through Concourse A.[21]

Artists would work side by side architects and engineers from the outset in planning new construction. Who took the lead would shift from one area to another, according to the imperatives of function and potential for "richness."[22] The artists would replace

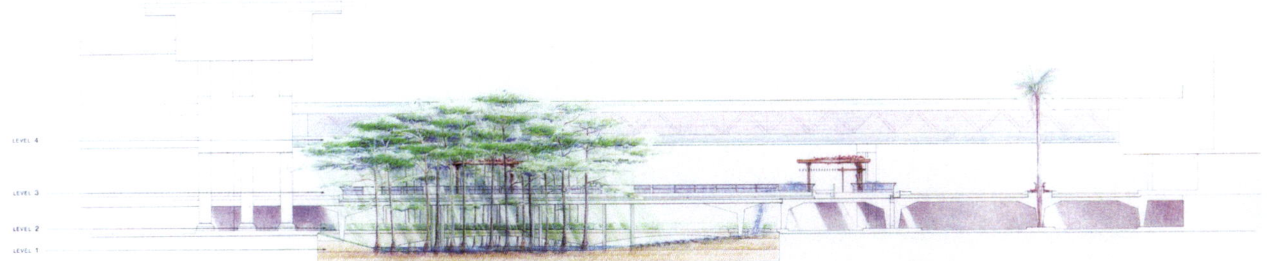

Robert Irwin, *Arts Enrichment Master Plan, proposed 1986 (unrealized)*, Miami International Airport, Central Park Garden, Section View, 1987. Color pencil on paper. Art in Public Places, Miami-Dade County Department of Cultural Affairs.

"indifference" with "attention," offering a "second layer of quality information" to Dick Judy,[23] the innovative and decisive director of the airport. The "qualitative" and the "quantitative" were both "real"[24] and would operate in "dialectical tension."[25] "While we all recognize the primacy of the logistical in setting airport policy and in all airport decision-making," Irwin reasoned, "it is in the measure of the actual give and take between the quantitative/bottom line criteria and the qualitative/enrichment criteria that we can first identify (see) the actual degree and character of our values."[26]

"That's the key," Irwin explained to Lawrence Weschler.

> Artists need to be in there from the start, making the argument for quality. The key to this thing, for example, is if you give an engineer a set of criteria which does not include a quality quotient, as it were—that is, if this sense of the quality, the character of the place is not a part of his original motivation—he will then basically put the road straight down the middle. He has no reason whatsoever to curve it. But if I can convince him that quality is absolutely a worthwhile thing and we can then work out a way in which the road can be efficient and also wander down by the river, then we have essentially both—he provides quality in the sense that the road works, I provide quality in that it passes by the river. Now in that way it essentially gets built into the criteria from the start rather than being added on afterwards. ... Now, if you look around and ask yourself who in this society is trained to make this argument for quality, the only ones that I can think of are artists. We're the only ones with no other real rationale for being except developing aesthetics or quality—we have no other function.[27]

Irwin made elaborate charts of every concourse, along with drawings of the airport as a whole, structuring the planning process around opportunities and problems, and the distinct perspectives and agendas at work. In the "Episodic Flow Chart," zones outlined in red require *clarity*. Zones marked in orange indicate locations of *security* operations. It

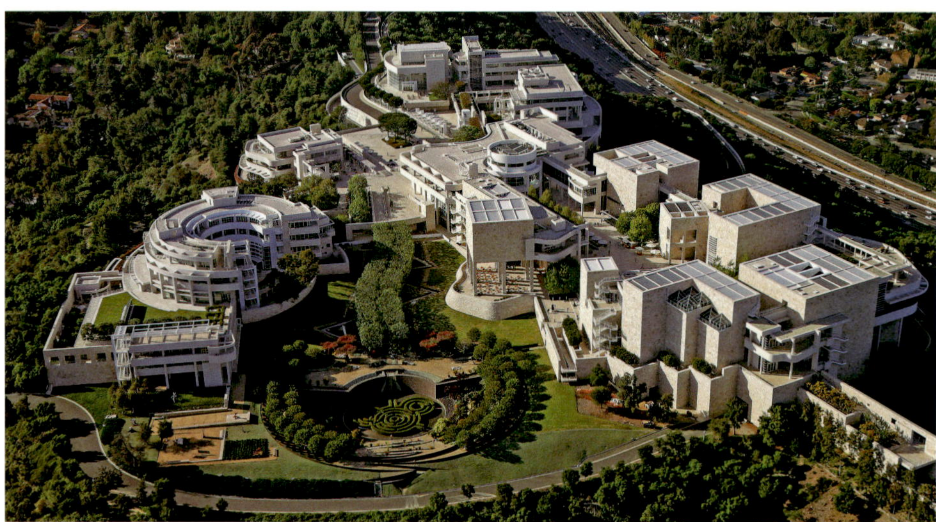

Aerial view of the Getty Center, Los Angeles, California, 2012.

is in Zones 2, 4, 7, 8, 11, and 12, outlined in blue or green, that *richness* can forge the way. Passages of the entry drive, together with much of the terminal itself and areas at the far end of each concourse, are prime for "richness." Zones delineated in green include the "Central Park" and an area of each concourse where an atrium or garden could be included (plate 6).

Arrival and departure by car, taxi, shuttle or bus would unfold in five "parts"—each with "a unique sense of place" clearly demarcated "one from the other"—but collectively conveying "a clear sense of progression ... as parts as well as a whole."[28] It was here that Irwin made his own proposal as an artist for the airport, preparing a separate, detailed *Ground Transportation Improvement Project* document, along with an array of drawings and plans. The design concept for an "Episodic Master Plan" was once again built around the "perceptual events" of "arrival – passage – seeking – finding – waiting – leaving."[29]

The ground transportation plan is made vivid in Irwin's plan view (plate 7). At far right of the drawing, Le Jeune Road Interchange requires clarity. In this first part of the approach to the airport, the "enrichment (sculpture) is in the design of the spiraling ramps of the traffic interchange and the shaped embankments."[30] Beyond the interchange, Central Boulevard is visually enclosed in vegetation, with swamp trees standing in a placid river to the north. The traveler emerges from this "green tunnel" that is the second zone of the entry drive, into the airy openness denoted in the aqueous blue areas. Curving ramps and crossovers flow through this third realm of the plan—a vista of causeways, water, sand, reeds and grasses, veiled in mist created by a grid of rain birds (plate 10). From here the traveler either drives onward to the terminal or heads to the parking structure, passing through the toll plaza—a tensile "curvilinear space frame"[31] that is the gateway from this evocative landscape (plate 9).

Irwin revamped the beleaguered garage as an efficient, clear, even vibrant and adventuresome space. Openings that would cut through the parking structures could be cast as "vertical Atrium pedestrian passageways" through which travelers would float on moving sidewalks, sheltered in the cool green light filtered through a tension fabric above. A floating garden of tropical plants would create a fantastical surround[32] in this fourth passage of the ground transportation scheme. The garages—north and south—would be color-coded (green,

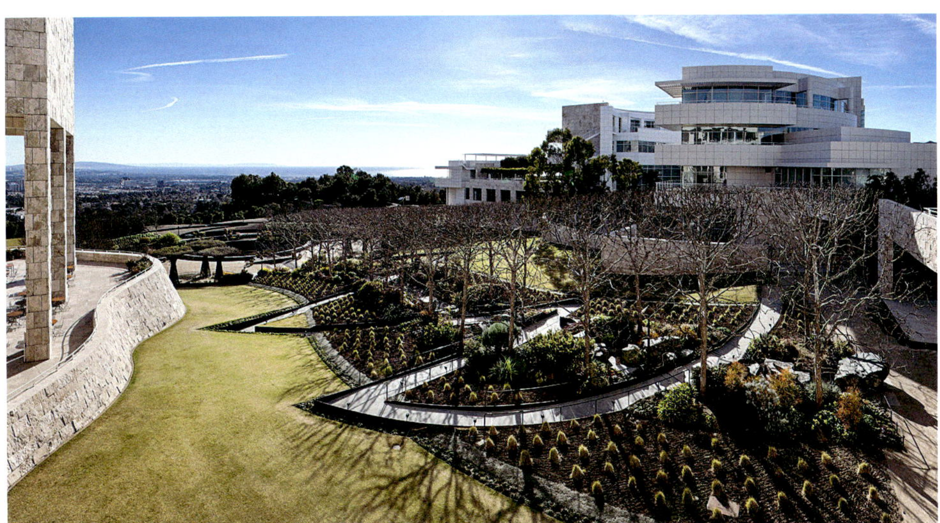

Robert Irwin. Getty Center Central Garden, Overview.

blue and violet to the north, orange, red and magenta to the south), enlisting a "lighting and painting program" as well as various alphanumerical and graphic symbols to orient the traveler (plates 8 and 14).[33]

The fifth, and culminating part of the ground transportation plan was the "Central Park." With VIP parking moved to a new structure to the east and the bus loop re-routed, Irwin had carved out space between the garage and terminal for a lush oasis in the center of the bustling airport. It was in the central park—"the pivotal gesture underwriting the whole arts enrichment ambition"[34]—that the individual "worlds" created by artists across the airport, and the journey of arrival and departure choreographed by Irwin, would click into place as parts of a whole. In the plans, the airport radiates from this core: toward the terminal and its concourses to the west; and the parking, roadways and passages of landscape to the east. A grove of cypresses would emerge from a shallow pool of water. Washingtonia palm trees would rise from the garden through openings cut in the medians of the upper drive. Two—maybe three—waterfalls would lend drama, veiling the juncture between roadway and garden.[35]

Visitors would encounter the central park from multiple levels and vantage points, most often on the drive approaching and departing the terminal. Floating walkways and people-movers at the upper levels traversed the garden between the garage and terminal—"the sense of floating through the space on the moving sidewalk is the grand experience."[36] And, for those with time, there would be a "promenade" on the garden's upper level—"a warm sun drenched urban sub-tropical plaza"[37]—with places to sit and to stroll, even to grab a snack. With arbors of bougainvillea and canopies shaped like leaves or bell-like flowers, the lush colors, textures and smells of tropical flowering plants would be engrossing. From the lower level, where the garden would typically be seen from a car or the sidewalk, the stand of cypresses would visually elide with the low ceiling to suggest a canopy-shaded retreat. The waterfalls would dampen the noise and aerate the air, which would vent through the openings for the palm trees in the medians above (plates 11–13 and 15).[38]

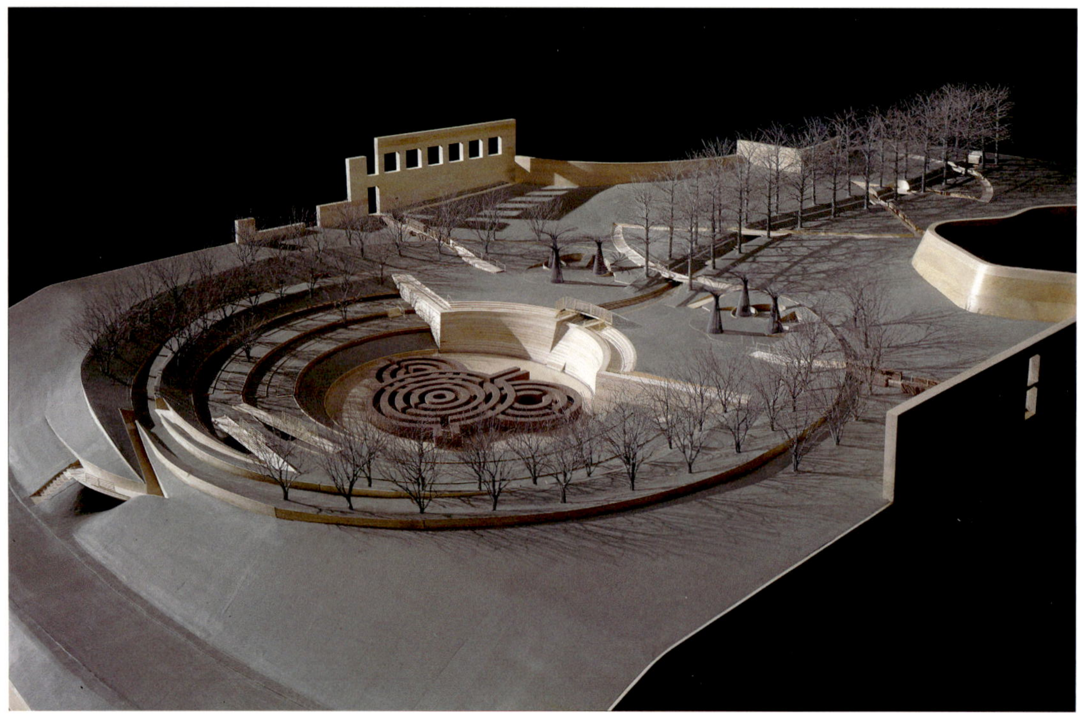

Model of the Getty Center *Central Garden*, 1994. Getty Research Institute, Special Collections, Robert Irwin papers (940081).

The case that Irwin had made for the largest-scale permanent project he had thus far tackled, in one of the most public of places, proved compelling. Dick Judy was convinced: a January 1987 Aviation Department report calls for the demolition of the "Park 1" garage to make way for "a park-like space which will convey to the traveler a lush tropical image of Miami … a 'people space.' "[39] By February 1987, the Professional Advisory Committee, which reported to the Metro-Dade Art in Public Places Trust, had endorsed Irwin's plan and "recommended proceeding immediately with its development."[40] Cesar Trasoberes, director of Art in Public Places, had been on board from the start.[41] Yet the process of putting the plan into action was stymied by structural impasses. While Irwin's timelines had been conceived to stay ahead of the airport's rapid-fire design and construction schedules, there was no way around the fact that the airport made decisions "at 70 mph" and the arts people considerably more slowly.[42] The budgets of Art in Public Places and the airport operated under distinct governmental agencies and regulations. The complexity of the evolving plan outstripped the administrative resources that were in-hand to negotiate the intricate process.

But the key question had been answered: from Dick Judy's vantage point, the "second layer" of information that Irwin had offered was invaluable. Acknowledging the logistical demands of the airport, Irwin had deployed a strategy of "dialectical tension" to interweave qualitative richness with quantitative necessity. The central park and the places of pause and passage created by artists throughout the airport would insinuate perceptual alertness, as well as clarity and order.[43] The hectic experience of the airport had been reframed to unfold episodically, the confusing agglomeration of spaces recast to make sense as parts to a whole. A political skirmish led Judy to retire in May 1989, and Irwin's Miami airport project was shelved. But the "case study" had laid the groundwork for possibilities soon to come.

• • •

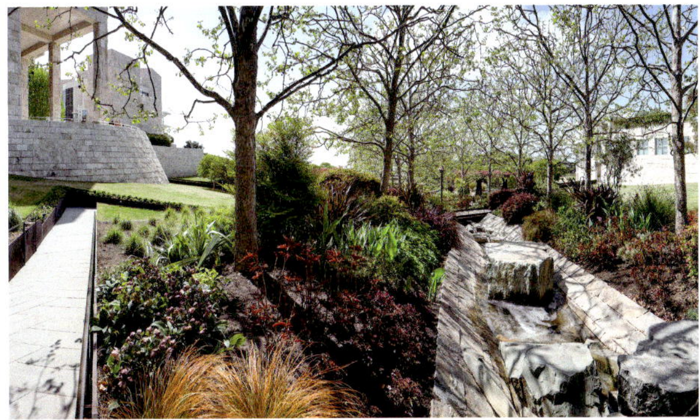

Robert Irwin, Getty Center *Central Garden*, Stream Garden.

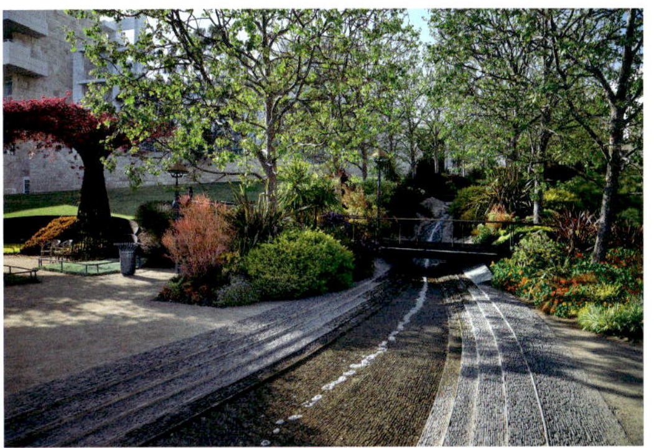

Robert Irwin, Getty Center *Central Garden*, Terrace Garden.

When Irwin received the invitation to propose a plan for the Getty Center's central garden in 1992, ground had already been broken for the buildings that Richard Meier had spent the better part of a decade envisioning. While the scenario surely augured a clash of wills (Meier had already developed his own design for the garden), here was a context that would allow Irwin to put into play the experience of scale and complexity gathered in Miami. The unfurling passages of landscape at the airport—from Le Jeune Circle to the central park—offered a backdrop for the unfolding of the garden at the Getty, which operates in site-determined response to the dramatic setting and commanding architecture. Kurt Forster (then the director of the Getty Research Institute) described the lay of the land: "[T]he architectural qualities of the Getty buildings will set up an almost overwhelming contrast to their surroundings, because they suggest *one* dominant relationship to the land at large: viewed from the Getty site, everything else will appear to be *dominated*, everything else will be beneath it, and *beheld at a distance*."[44] The site for the garden was expansive, its several acres framed by the Getty Museum and Getty Research Institute.

Spotting the garden from the plaza above, the visitor is drawn down the stairs toward a stream.
> One of the elements of the garden is this process of enticing and pulling you down. Your first view of it, of course, from up here or one of the other vista points, is as this really strong graphic element. ... That's what supplies much of the scale of the garden, as up against the grand scale of the surrounding architecture. ... [T]he path itself draws you down to the plaza, and the plaza then lets you look down on the bowl, and then, hopefully, you have the desire to want to descend into the bowl. So the whole thing is a series of descents, becoming, in a sense, more intimate as you go along.[45]

The zigzagging path of arcs and straight lines runs along the stream, juts out beyond the allée of sycamores into the deer grass, then cuts back into the realm of coursing water and the "tapestry" of plants. The herringbone-patterned Pennsylvania bluestone of the path yields to herringbone-patterned teak at the five bridges that cross over the water at intervals. The patina of these materials—like the bronze handrails and grates, and the Cor-Ten steel that defines the switchbacks of the path—will deepen in time (plates 18 and 19).[46]

This entry stroll along the stream alerts the visitor to the sensory surround. Subtle shifts unfold in the color and height of the plantings (more gray at the start, becoming increasingly vibrant as the path descends). The arrangement of green chert rock in the stream is "muscular" and packed at the top of the slope, gradually opening up, before finally leaving the water to ripple across the stone stream bed as the path nears the bougainvillea plaza.

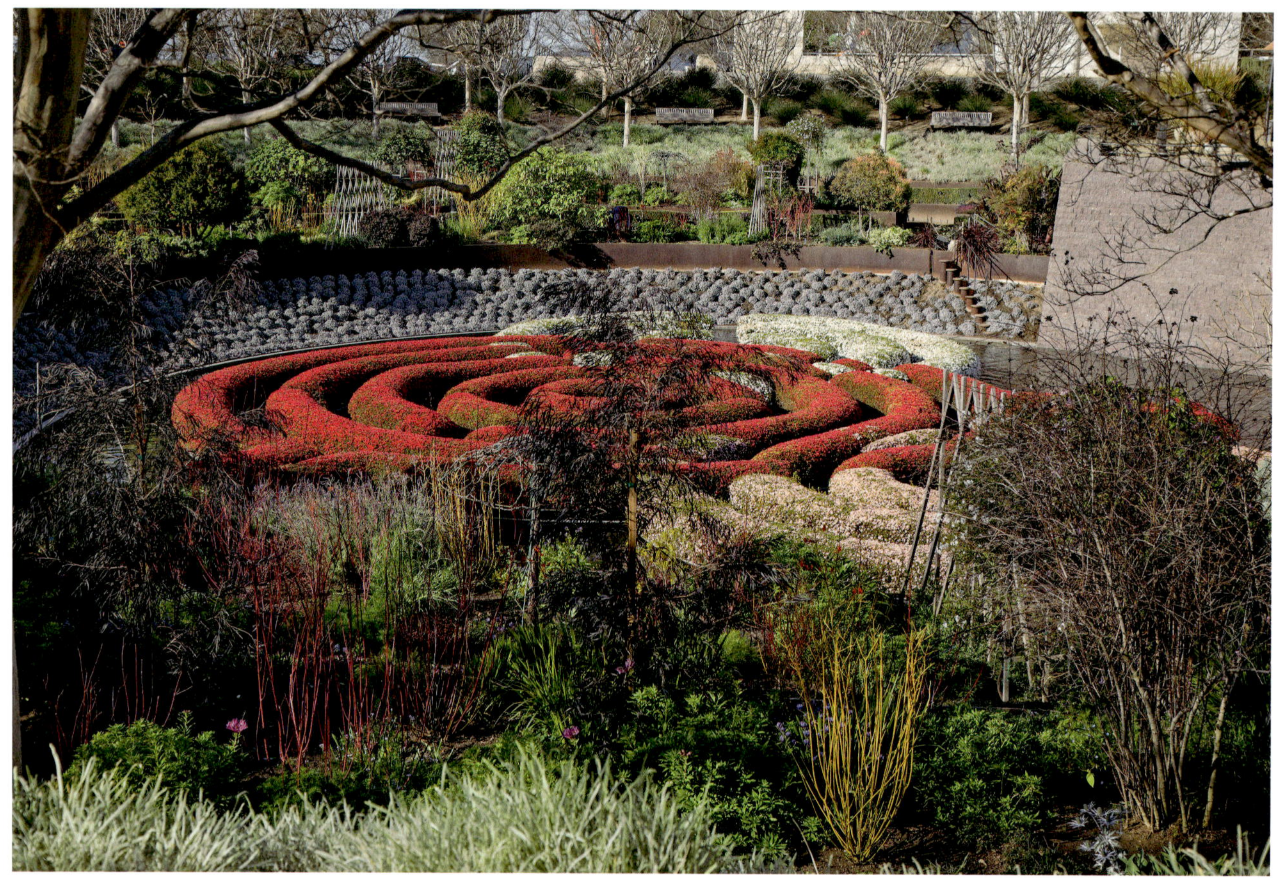

Robert Irwin, Getty Center *Central Garden*, Bowl Garden.

The timbre and tone of the stream are carefully tuned by the scale and placement of boulders, rocks and stones.[47]

Attuned to nuance in the shaded enclosure of the stream path—where the palette is based on the structure, color and texture of plants and leaves, and where grays and greens predominate—the visitor emerges into the radiance of the bougainvillea plaza. The vista to the south opens beyond, stretching to the Pacific horizon. Six arbors, crafted from rebar, are lush with red, magenta, orange and white bougainvillea (plates 21 and 22). The bluestone path yields to the earthen tones of decomposed granite in this plaza and the paths beyond. Running under an arched bridge, the stream reappears as a falls down the carnelian-granite "chadar" wall, the drop in elevation recalling the terrain of the canyon that once occupied the space. As the visitor descends a curve of steps, or crosses the bridge of this luminous bougainvillea terrace, the azalea maze, unseen until now—with its intersecting circles of apple blossom, hino-crimson, and snow azaleas[48]—startlingly materializes within the circular pool into which the waterfall flows. A bowl of exorbitantly colored flowers radiates outward from the pool.

Walkways lead the visitor around the top of the bowl—with its two encircling rows of crape myrtle trees—to enter from the south along paths and bridges that echo the Cor-Ten-lined switchbacks of the stream garden. "At the center of the first bridge is a space Irwin calls the

'Power Spot.' Here is the central axis of the garden: amazing flower beds on each side, the azalea pool below, the waterfall directly ahead, and the Stream Garden in the distance, a series of rings radiating out to the surrounding beauty of the architecture."[49] Moving down into the flower garden, the viewer is enveloped by the arcing Cor-Ten profiles of the entry paths to the south—which close off the vista and complete the bowl—and absorbed in the colors, textures, smells, sounds, "feelings"[50] of this exuberant, intricate realm.

The bowl garden is both rigorously structured and luxuriant. The purple ring just above the azalea pool "is *Kalanchoe pumila* ... ."

> Now, May or June, depending on the weather, the kalanchoe will fade out, and the next ring up, the tulbaghia, will go into full bloom and become a solid ring of color. And then in midsummer, the trees, the crape myrtles, on the circling path above them, will go into bloom. So that the color rises up from the pool, a ring at a time, from March to the end of the summer.[51]

Effulgent colors and textures prevail: yarrow, asters, heather, black-eyed susans, germander sage, clover, nasturtiums, dahlias, heliotrope, sweet peas, trumpeter, iceberg and dublin bay roses, to name just a few.[52] "The Getty Central Garden is a sculpture ... in the form of a garden ... that aspires to be art. In this key sense the planting of the garden is like a painting, not so much concerned with species & origin, as with color, texture & conditioned relations."[53] And it is here that the garden culminates—not only as a "go-for-broke flower garden,"[54] but in its capacity to induce a quieter kind of wonder, as the visitor pays attention to the delicate beauty of the petals of a flower, the intricate architecture of a leaf, a startling juxtaposition of colors, or the song of a finch heard against the falls.

In the model made in 1994, the structure of the garden is clear. The geometries of the paths, bougainvillea plaza, azalea maze, and bowl; the allée of sycamores flanking the stream; and the stands of crape myrtles that reiterate the radiating circles of the bowl garden are all in place. During winter, the garden more closely approximates the clarity of the model. "This is when you see all the stuff, not just the trees, that I did to establish the so-called bones of the place," Irwin has noted. "But all of that in turn allows me to do the opposite in summer. ... At that point I will allow the garden to obliterate the boundaries, to ignore all the geometry and go for complete exuberance ... ."[55]

"The actual site of this garden," Irwin has observed, "is deeply embedded in a surrounding architecture committed to a formal geometry."

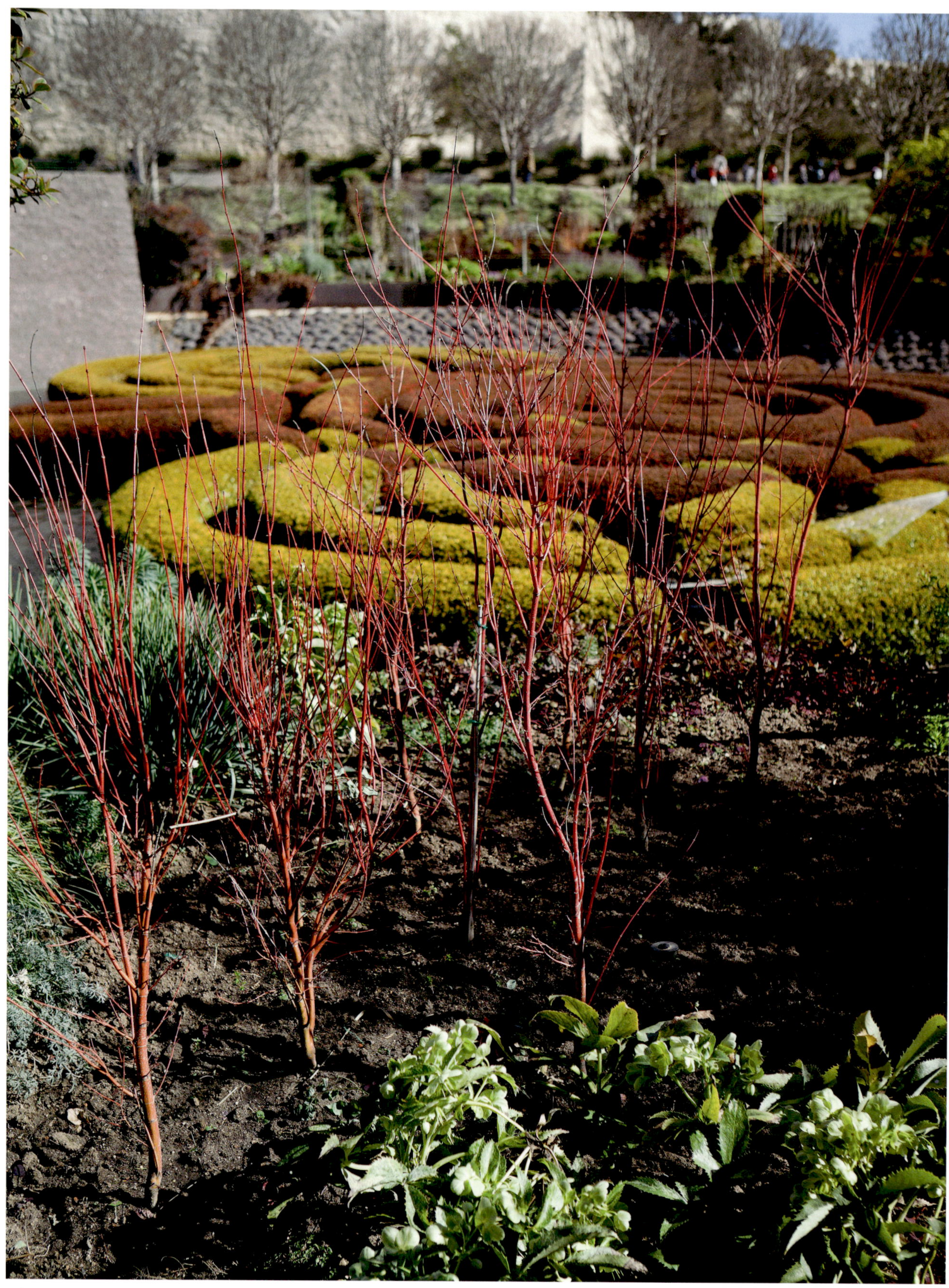

Robert Irwin, Getty Center *Central Garden*, Bowl Garden.

To create the transition from the formidable scale of the architecture to the necessary intimacy of a garden ... the plan of the sculpture responds to this condition both in the scale of its main gestures ... and in that every element in the garden begins with a simple geometry, which in most cases is compounded to first be seen and understood as pattern and in many cases compounded even further to be experienced tactilely as textures.[56]

The drawings and models for the *Central Garden* served at once to clarify and communicate the plan. But what cannot, of course, be conveyed by a drawing is the shifting and ephemeral character of the garden. And so the drawings lay out the schema across which the evanescent might be "courted"[57] in the thickness of the world.

• • •

If the possibilities of both the Miami airport project and the Getty garden were determined by their sites, then, too, Irwin calibrated the visitor's experience as an unfolding over time. While the journey through the airport was conceived episodically and the "richness" that was "threaded in" replaced "indifference" with "attention," the Getty garden was composed as an intricately wrought perceptual continuum.

The sole criterion of this sculpture/garden is the experience of beauty ... as a nice place to be ... it is my feeling that most of our interest in art begins with our having had, at one time, a very special aesthetic experience ... which inspires each of us individually to want to know more. It is in this sense that the sole ambition of this sculpture/garden is to create the possibility of just such a moment.[58]

If the wonder is in the experience, then the snare is in the plan, which choreographs the encounter with the beautiful. The drawings and models for Miami International Airport and the Getty *Central Garden* lay this out. If "seeing is the initial act of valuing, and the nature and infinite potential of human beings to see and to aesthetically order the world is the *one pure subject of art*," then "art capable of real social meaning—change—is art capable of manifesting a new set of values."[59] In a realm that is "ever changing"—"never twice the same"[60]—we "set in motion our desires for how we want things to be ... and in turn discover how things actually are ... and then we learn to work at keeping them in play."[61]

Notes

Interviews are with the author, in San Diego, except as otherwise noted.

1 Robert Irwin, "The Hidden Structures of Art," in *Robert Irwin*, ed. Russell Ferguson (Los Angeles, CA: Museum of Contemporary Art, 1993), 42.

2 Irwin, foreword to *Plants in the Getty's Central Garden* by Jim Duggan (Los Angeles, CA: J. Paul Getty Museum, 2003), ix.

3 Irwin, "The Hidden Structures of Art," 18, 33; interview with Irwin, summer 1992; Irwin, *Being and Circumstance: Notes Toward a Conditional Art* (Larkspur Landing, CA: Lapis Press, 1985), 14, 24–25.

4 Irwin, in *Robert Irwin: The Beauty of Questions*, directed by Leonard Feinstein (University of California Extension Center for Media and Independent Learning, 1997), DVD; interview with Irwin, 2005.

5 Ibid; interview with Irwin, fall 1991; Irwin, "The Hidden Structures of Art," 39–40.

6 Interview with Irwin, 2004.

7 Ibid.

8 Irwin, in Lawrence Weschler and Robert Irwin, "This Petal, That Stalk: A Series of Garden Walks," in Lawrence Weschler, *Robert Irwin—Getty Garden* (Los Angeles, CA: J. Paul Getty Museum, 2002), 32.

9 Irwin, "The Hidden Structures of Art," 23.

10 Irwin in Lawrence Weschler, "In a Desert of Pure Feeling," *New Yorker*, June 7, 1993, 90.

11 Irwin in Duggan, *Plants in the Getty's Central Garden*, viii, ix.

12 Interview with Irwin, 2004; see also Lawrence Weschler, "Playing It As It Lays & Keeping It In Play: A Visit with Robert Irwin," in *Robert Irwin*, 161.

13 See Robert Irwin, *Arts Enrichment Master Plan, proposed 1986 (unrealized), Miami International Airport, Airport Experience (First Presentation)*, 1986. Getty Research Institute, Los Angeles, Special Collections, Robert Irwin papers (940081) tube 26; see also Irwin, "Arts Enrichment Master Plan: Miami International Airport," 1986, 1–2, Robert Irwin Papers, 1970–2004, Getty Research Institute [GRI], Los Angeles, (research library accession no. 940081).

14 Irwin, "Arts Enrichment Master Plan," 5, 18.

15 Ibid, 33–34, 37, 13–15.

16 Ibid, 29–31.

17 Ibid, 49.

18 Ibid, 1.

19 Interview with Irwin, 2004.

20 Irwin, "Arts Enrichment Master Plan," 43; Irwin, Presentation to the Professional Advisory Committee, September 21, 1987, videotape, Metro-Dade Art in Public Places records.

21 Matthew Simms, *Robert Irwin: A Conditional Art* (New Haven, CT and London: Yale University Press, 2016), 196–97.

22 Ibid, 187.

23 Irwin, "Arts Enrichment Master Plan," 1–2.

24 Interview with Irwin, 2004.

25 Interview with Irwin, 2004; Irwin, "Arts Enrichment Master Plan," 3. Psychologist Ed Wortz and architect Coy Howard were key in thinking through the airport with Irwin.

26 Irwin, "Program: Park I," Robert Irwin Papers, GRI.

27 Irwin, quoted in Weschler, "Playing It As It Lays," 163–64.

28 Robert Irwin, "Arts Enrichment Aesthetic Program—Ground Transportation
   Improvement Project [Miami International Airport]," 1986, 1, Robert Irwin Papers, GRI.

29 Ibid.

30 Ibid, 2.

31 Ibid, 3–5.

32 Ibid, 7.

33 Irwin, "Garage Reorganization Project Proposal—Miami International Airport Arts
   Enrichment Program," 1–5, Robert Irwin Papers, GRI.

34 Irwin, "Ground Transportation Improvement Project," 8.

35 Interview with Irwin, 2005.

36 Irwin, "Ground Transportation Improvement Project," 8.

37 Ibid, 11.

38 Ibid, 10; interview with Irwin, 2005.

39 Rick Bejarano, Project Status Report: Ground Transportation Improvements Program,
   January 7, 1987, 3, 5–6, Miami International Airport records; interview with Dick Judy,
   Cedar Key, Florida, 2005.

40 Minutes of Professional Advisory Committee Meeting, February 21, 1987, 3, Robert Irwin
   Papers, GRI.

41 Interview with Cesar Trasoberes, Miami, 2004. Trasoberes' predecessor, Patricia Fuller,
   had been crucial in setting the stage.

42 Interview with Irwin, 2004.

43 Irwin, "Arts Enrichment Master Plan," 46–50.

44 Lawrence Weschler, "When Fountainheads Collide: Robert Irwin at Richard Meier's
   Getty" (1997) in Weschler, *Seeing Is Forgetting the Name of the Thing One Sees* (Berkeley,
   CA: University of California Press, 2008), 237–60; *Concert of Wills: Making the Getty
   Center* (Maysles Films Inc., 2003); Kurt Forster, Memorandum of March 7, 1992, Robert
   Irwin Papers, GRI.

45 Irwin, "This Petal, That Stalk," 31.

46 Ibid, 41, 79; Duggan, *Plants in the Getty's Central Garden*, 33.

47 Irwin, "This Petal, That Stalk," 41; Duggan, *Plants in the Getty's Central Garden*, 19.

48 Irwin, "This Petal, That Stalk," 97; Duggan, *Plants in the Getty's Central Garden*, 29, 112.

49 Duggan, *Plants in the Getty's Central Garden*, 30.

50 Irwin, "This Petal, That Stalk," 35.

51 Ibid, 114.

52 Duggan, *Plants in the Getty's Central Garden*, 48–128.

53 Irwin, "Getty Garden," in *Notes Toward a Conditional Art*, ed. Matthew Simms
   (Los Angeles, CA: J. Paul Getty Museum, 2011), 324.

54 Irwin "This Petal, That Stalk," 119.

55 Ibid, 33.

56 Irwin, "Getty Garden," 324.

57 Irwin, "This Petal, That Stalk," 63, 66.

58 Irwin, "Getty Garden," 324.

59 See Irwin, "The Hidden Structures of Art," 23, 41.

60 Irwin, Getty Garden inscription, in Duggan, *Plants in the Getty's Central Garden*, viii.

61 Irwin in Duggan, *Plants in the Getty's Central Garden*, ix.

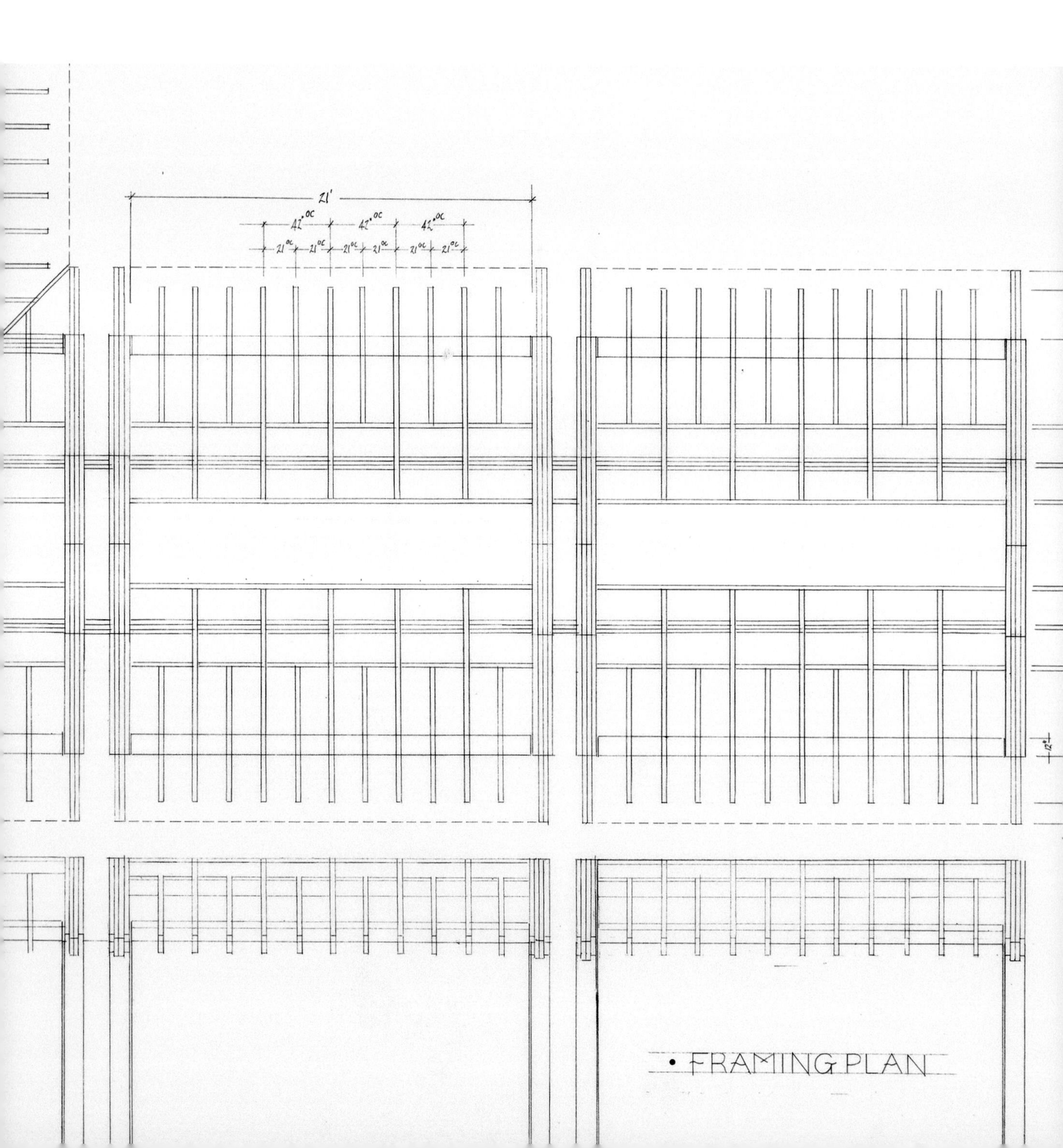

21'
42" oc
42" oc
42" oc
21" oc
21" oc
21" oc
21" oc
21" oc
21" oc

• FRAMING PLAN

THE REST IS ALL SKY: Irwin in Marfa

Ed Schad

The area of the Chihuahuan desert that lies north of the Rio Grande and west of the Pecos River is called the Trans-Pecos territory. Its array of pans and mountains were formed through a series of volcanic events 35,000,000 years ago, followed by more modest volcanism for 18,000,000 years. Walk it, and you'll find yucca, chihuahua scurfpea, bushy wild-buckwheat, beargrass, sotol, blue grama, and spanish dagger. One won't walk very far without water.

Marfa, Texas, population 2,000, sits near the burned-out caldera of the Paisano Volcano, a remnant of which rests to the east of the town. As you drive into Marfa southeast on Texas State Highway 90, you enter one of the Trans-Pecos's many basins, a semi-desert terrain bordered by the Davis Mountains along the northeast ridge, with the Chinati Mountains forming a curved border southwest. These mountains look sparse on the horizon, less cohesive ranges than an association of isolated mountains, all separate and individual, bound by a common climate. But they are formidable. Some reach high enough, in fact, to form their own ecosystems, micro-climates known as *sky islands*.

"There's something about being here," Robert Irwin has said of the area. "You're driving down I-10, and it's kind of dull. Then the minute you hit Van Horn and turn right and start to drop down, the whole thing changes, and it's kind of magical. It stands up and hums."[1]

Marfa is the type of place where ranchers go when they say they are "headed into town," meaning it's home to groceries, gas, supplies, and a wonderful 1886 Second Empire courthouse, the county seat for surrounding Presidio County. The town began as a railroad watering spot and is built around that same railroad track, which roughly bisects it. Its grid is not a true-south orientation, which may have worked well in a time before air conditioning, both to lessen the intensity of the sun through a house's windows, and also to regulate the light such that one side of the house was not completely in shadow at certain times during the day.

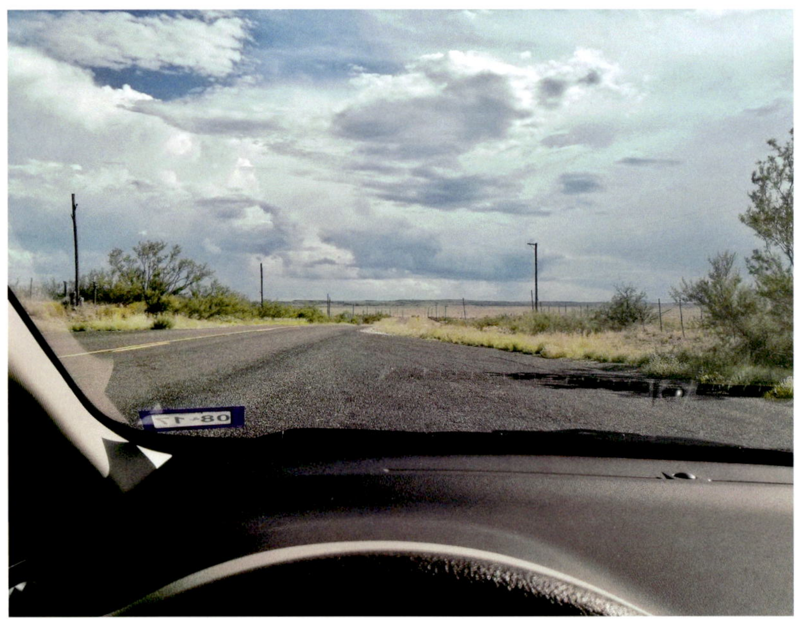

View from author's windshield, Ranch Road, Marfa, Texas, 2016.

The sun leaves its mark everywhere in Marfa. People in the street can be seen a little too clearly, meaning that they also see you too clearly. Stick your fingers in the pockmarks of a fallen piece of adobe, and you'll find dirt and straw turning to dust. Downtown, the buildings along Highland Street are painted an immodest white, which doubles down on the sun and sears your eyes at mid-day. One of these buildings is actually called the "Brite Building," forming an unintentional but appropriate pun. This flat-fronted structure, punctuated with spanish tile accents, contains Donald Judd's old office, full of a magnificent collection of furniture, work tables, and art. Light floods in through the windows. It's as hot as a sauna in the summer.

Marfa's layout, originally planned at an angle to the cardinal directions (what look like later developments see the grid turned back to north/south), makes for two, now very visible features of the town, striking in their alignment to a north/south axis: Donald Judd's *15 untitled works in concrete*, a concrete sculpture one-kilometer long to the south of town, probably still as strange and striking as the day it was unveiled; and an old military hospital, perhaps at a five-or-so-degree tilt from the axis, now re-made by Robert Irwin into *Untitled (dawn to dusk)*.

Writing about Irwin's hospital requires paying attention to everything that surrounds and informs the hospital—everything that runs up to and out from it. Volcanoes and sky islands, hardscrabble Texas grass and scraggly bushes, army camps and borders, corridors and windows, the hard sun emerging from a soft morning—the same sun dissolving into the delights of evening—are all part of the Irwin hospital. An installation by Irwin is about orientation, as in the determination of one's relative position to an environment, especially their position as *part of* and *embedded in* the reality of the environment.

• • •

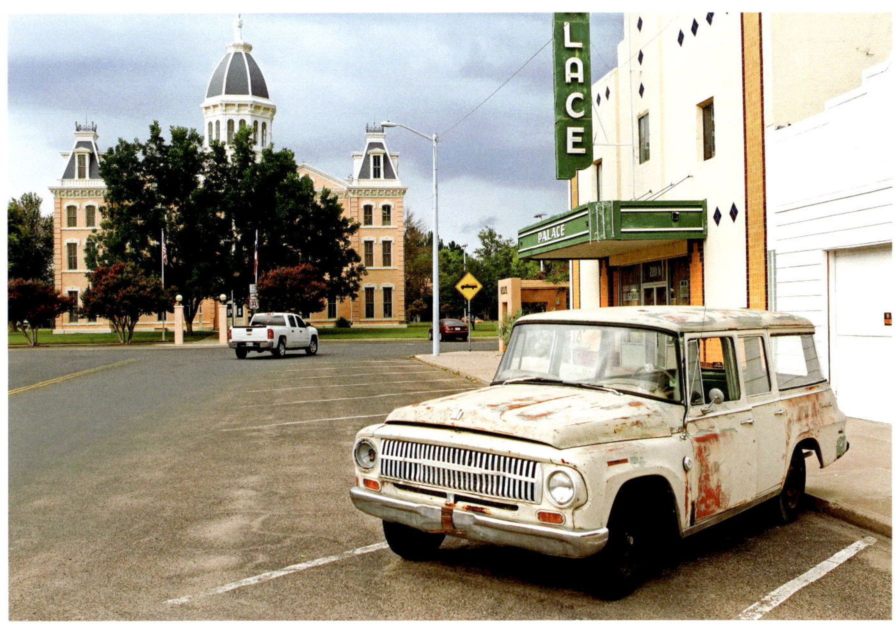

Downtown Marfa, Texas, 2015.

A simple gesture will do, as long it is conveyed in correct manner. I remember being involved with an Irwin long before I even knew what it was, driving through *Portal Park Slice* on Pearl Street in downtown Dallas. At first, all I knew was something had changed when I drove through that part of town. When I drove by those long strips of steel, it was like a flicker in the ordinary course of the day. I eventually had to figure it out—I had to know what it was. At the time, I had no interest in art. Irwin had reached me through perception, through relationships that he shared with me. All I had had to do was pay attention. An Irwin installation is far from something assertive, or something that marks its existence *against* an environment. Instead, the installation has to be *part* of the environment, part of the internal and established will of the environment, both natural and lived in by the people who inhabit it.

I arrived at *Untitled (dawn to dusk)*, as it happened, at dusk. I had never been to Chinati or Marfa before, and had just made the drive from El Paso. The Irwin installation was almost finished: sprinklers clicked and hissed around the C-shaped structure and its metal roof, and as I walked around it, I found a concrete-and-gravel walkway that split the property from Katherine Street to Bonnie Street. In the center of the walkway was a newly installed but old-looking assortment of basalt columns—a small echo, maybe, of the Giant's Causeway in Northern Ireland. The basalt holds the courtyard of the building in much the same way an obelisk would hold a piazza in Italy or the central pyramid would anchor an old Mayan ruin in Mexico. The basalt is surrounded by Cor-Ten steel garden boxes, silently rusting in the courtyard of the building, holding palo verde trees and native blue grama grass.

Inside the front door, right in the center, Jeff Jamieson, Irwin's longtime right hand and a master of everything, was supervising the fabrication of the many scrims of fabric that occupy the building. On the right side, four doorways were cut through four white scrims. On the left, four doorways were cut through four black scrims. I entered the white side through the four passageways into the south end, which opened into a long north/south corridor. In

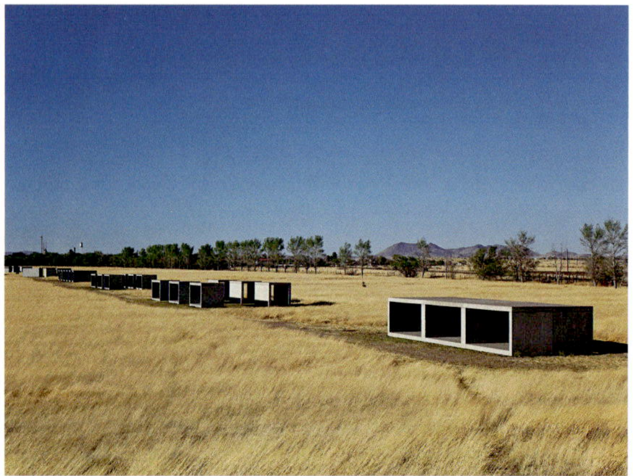

Donald Judd, *15 untitled works in concrete*, 1980–1984, detail.
2.5 x 2.5 x 5 meters. Permanent collection, the Chinati Foundation,
Marfa, Texas.

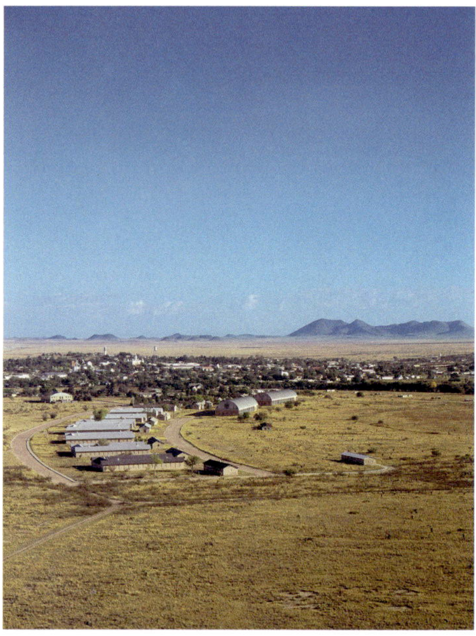

Aerial view of the Chinati Foundation, Marfa, Texas.

the center of the corridor, also running north/south, were two white scrims, side by side, running the length of the hall. Windows lined both walls on either side of the long scrims.

At 8 p.m., the sun was swiftly falling, the July heat accompanied by the sound of the sprinklers, still clicking, and light flooded through the rectangular windows, casting their images on the white center scrims like a series of vibrant monochrome paintings. A similar thing was happening on the opposite side, only on black scrims. I walked the south side, down and back through the scrim gateways, the light casting nets of window-sized impressions on the interior scrims and walls of the opposite corridors. The light increased in intensity as the sun fell, until the moment when the rectangles began to disperse across the scrims, blurring like a series of hovering Rothkos, growing ever lighter with the declining sun until only the scrims remained in their illusion of solidity. This was the beginning. Much would follow.

• • •

The installation took seventeen years from commission to completion, starting with a ruin of a military hospital, continuing through occasional controversy, and opening with a Chinati BBQ attended by far-flung art people as well as members of the Marfa community. But the hospital itself dates back to 1920, nine years after the establishment of the U.S. Cavalry encampment that originally occupied the property. Founded as an American patrol outpost to monitor the impact of Francisco Madero's burgeoning Mexican Revolution along the U.S. border, the camp expanded during World War I, and in World War II—by then renamed Fort D.A. Russell—joined twenty-six other military and prisoner-of-war camps dotted across Texas. In 1946, the hospital was decommissioned, along with the entire fort, beginning its slow decline into the ruin that Irwin would be given for his commission.

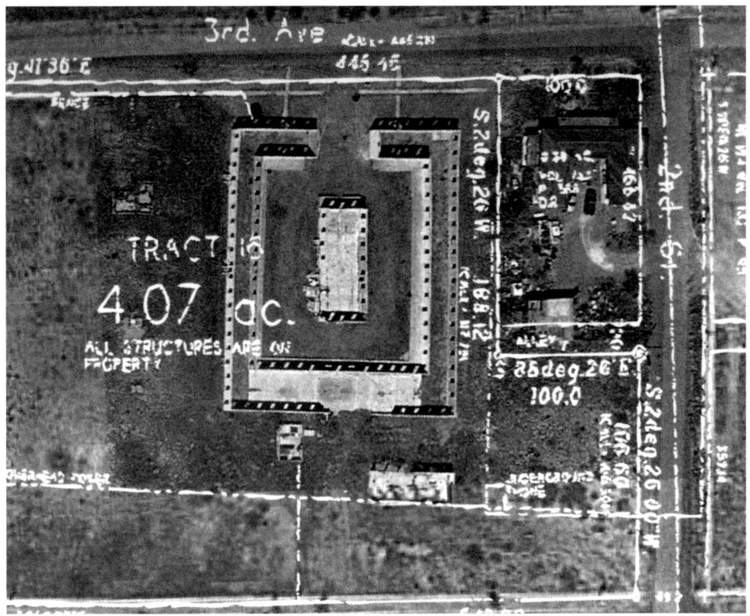

Aerial survey view of Fort D.A. Russell hospital building before construction.
Chinati Foundation archives, Marfa, Texas, "Robert Irwin project" box.

I grew up near Camp Howze, a similar military installation in North Texas, near the town of Gainesville. One doesn't have to be nostalgic to think that the camps are returning to the earth too quickly; one need only dwell for a moment on the complicated view the United States has of its own history—and its tendency to destroy its heritage. Camp Howze, for instance, is now just a series of gridded concrete piers that mark where the buildings once stood in the grass. I grew up with stories of Camp Howze, and was even gifted the occasional bullet casing that had been found near the old artillery ranges. (One day, as though it had become just an ordinary thing, my uncle brought an old unexploded mortar shell home. It lived menacingly next to my grandma's propane tank for years.)

I only bring up Camp Howze to, in a certain way, sympathize with the people who did not want to see the ruin of the Fort D.A. Russell hospital converted into some kind of artwork. There is romance to a ruin, a sense of the fleeting nature of history. However—and this is something important about the Irwin installation—a ruin is something more than just a temporary marker of human movements across a mere blink of historical circumstance. A ruin reveals something essential about the landscape and the reality that is working upon it. A ruin points to a deeper movement.

As I experienced the installation, Irwin answered my questions about the loss of the historical ruin before I even was able to ask them out loud: What would it mean, for instance, for a ruin to contain history but not be reduced to it? What would it mean for a ruin to keep what is most essential, yet open itself up to become an enhanced channel of those essentials? How could one conjure the ruin without building its copy, like some gift shop in Colonial Williamsburg? Could a ruin tilt the world to demonstrate how a landscape influences and drives the micro events of history—how basic conditions of volcanoes and wind and sun organize our borders, partially determine what we fight over, and change us in ways far out of our view?

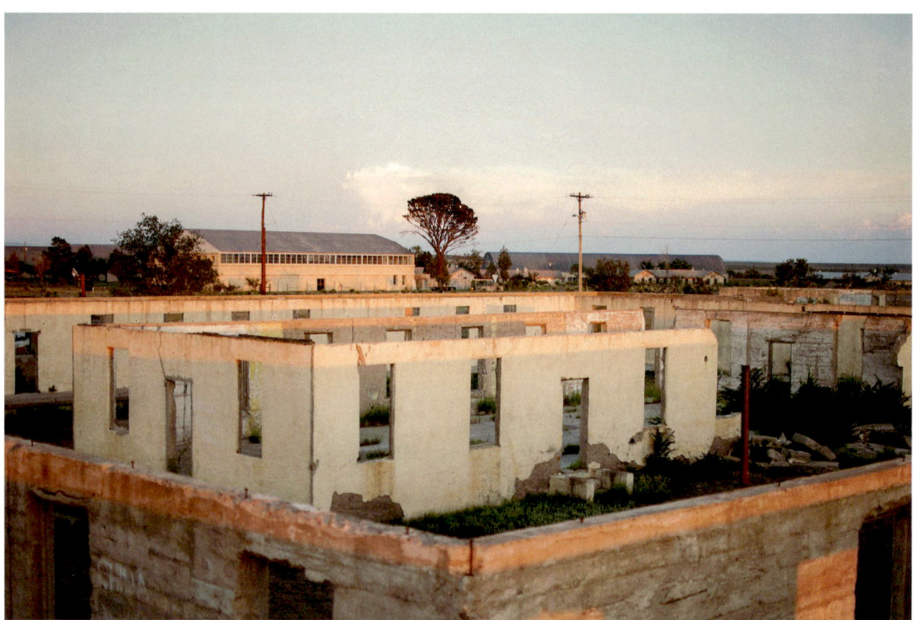

William Vizcarra, View of Fort D.A. Russell hospital building before construction, 2014.

A ruin, in a sense, works in a similar way as Irwin does as artist. Ruins do what the earth tells them to do. They have no human master or purpose. They simply are what they are, bending to the weather. A ruin's memory dissolves into the reality of its day-to-day life in nature. The environment shapes the frame for a ruin's existence rather than the other way around.

The hospital ruin in Marfa had so many things naturally going for it in the way of beauty, so many registers through which one could ponder the fort, the town, the landscape, and even the larger tectonic movements of earth. It seems that these are exactly the things that Irwin worked to keep, and works to find in every location he arrives at, whether it is the grounds of the Getty Center or a museum stairway. He only wants to show what is there—and in Marfa, he found a condition that was revealing the nature of its own reality, showing a set of conditions beyond the momentary circumstance of specific histories.

• • •

There is a photo of the early site that later became *Untitled (dawn to dusk)*, taken from slightly above the old hospital structure. In the photo, the ruin is alive to the sky and, quite literally, absorbing the area around it. The C-shaped structure had lost its roof, and you can see the shadows working down its plaster walls as though the building is a trap for the sun. The top of the walls are ablaze in creamy pinks, and the day takes the instant to throw those specific, unrepeatable colors. Nature has taken over through the tougher aspects of this perennially tough part of South Texas. The ground is speckled with broken bits of the structure, pulled slowly apart by the whip of rain and heat. The grass that grows in the ruin is the grass that had to grow there, which was in a position to grow there.

Irwin's preparatory drawings show a person getting to know these conditions. Some were present immediately: to keep the sky present and dynamic, to use much of the footprint of the original structure, to work with the existing center of the site, and to use materials that

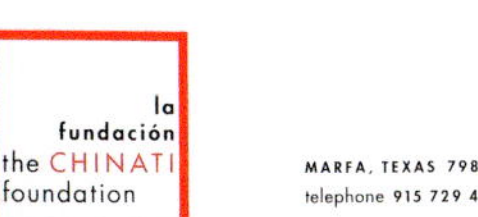

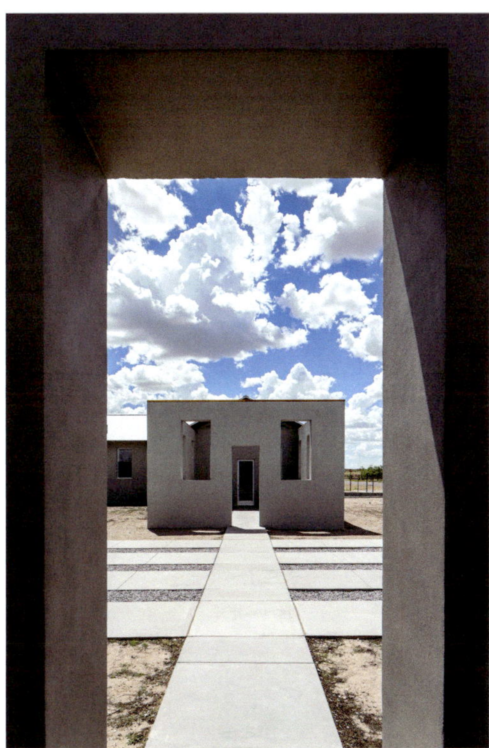

Letter from Marianne Stockebrand, Director of the Chinati Foundation, to Robert Irwin (undated, ca. late 1999).

Robert Irwin, *Untitled (dawn to dusk)*, 2016.

mostly matched the economic and military ethic of the original structure (plates 34–39). However, a gathering of conditions that are harder to see is also present: the early push for the sun to interact with color, the heightened sense of daily transition from dark to light, the strong central axis that directs the eye through the entire structure north into the mountains and south towards Big Bend. The approximate north/south orientation of the building meant an even progression of shadow and light. Its corridors spoke of passages and partially echoed, in both their size and structure, each of the other buildings at Chinati Foundation—including Irwin's earlier installation inside one of them, *Untitled (Four Walls)*—and therefore echoed the historic buildings of Fort D.A. Russell. Its C shape, and the position of its former inner building, gave it a wonderful center. The partial circle of the building, with its opening on one end, was not unlike the circle of mountains surrounding it, with its openings into other basins.

Color Glass (orange), Marfa Half-Plan and *Color Glass (violet), Marfa Half-Plan* show Irwin at work (plates 32 and 33). Like all Irwin installations, the drawings are a testament to understanding and seeing, an effort to move inside of an environment without getting in the way. On two sides are the windows as they existed in the original ruin, but Irwin has added slits in the walls for the light to flood through on the east and west sides. The roofs of these east and west buildings were to be topped with colored glass to filter the light through a progression of red/orange (to the west) and violet (to the east). On the north and south sides of the building, simple wooden roof structures are equipped with clear glass, opening the building to the sky in much the same way as the original ruin (plates 29 and 30).

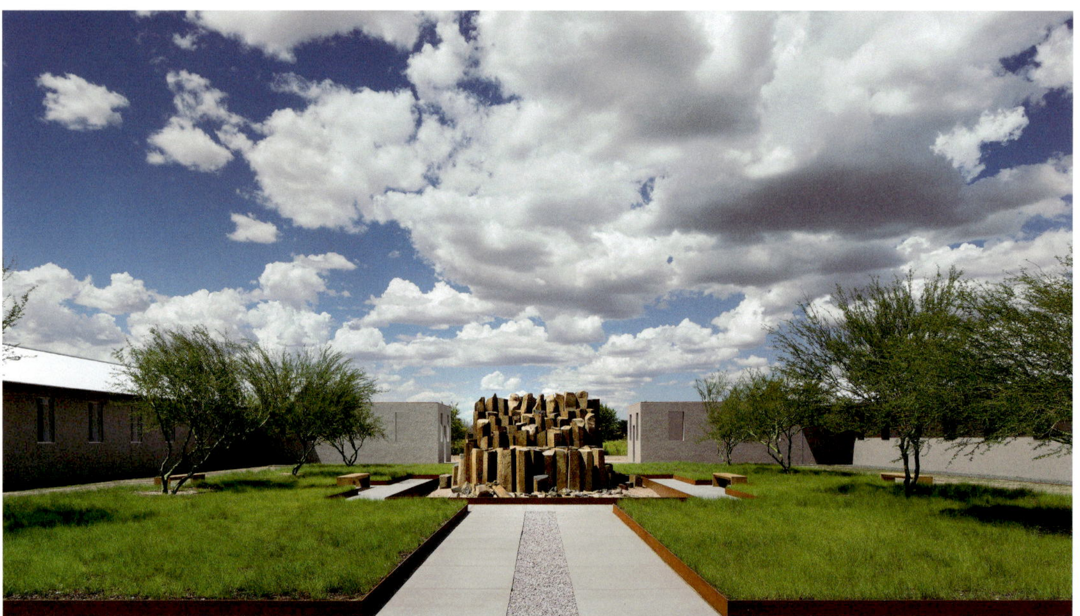

Robert Irwin, *Untitled (dawn to dusk)*, 2016.

As the plans move forward, the essentials of the ruin and the original hospital remain, but a refinement occurs; values present in the beginning become more subtle, more embedded into the reality of that part of Texas. The building becomes (at least on most of the exterior) an image of the original hospital. It has wooden rafters and a simple roof, it is made of plaster-covered concrete blocks. It gestures to the old ruin on the north ends of the east and west corridors with two small antechambers open to the sky. Color has disappeared from the glass, windows, and roof, and instead lives in the sun's natural day-to-day enthusiasms (especially if there is a little drama in the sky) (plates 46 and 49). Instead of a path running through the entire north/south axis, multiple footpaths run to a single point, the basalt marking the literal and physical history of the region as the result of a volcanic aftermath.

Through the use of scrims—a longtime material of Irwin's as the stuff of his interior installations—one sees Irwin the gardener at work in a profound way in Marfa. As in his projects for the Getty or the Los Angeles County Museum of Art, or even that concrete slice I experienced in Dallas, Irwin is mastering scale in Marfa, gathering up the conditions so those very conditions can be reflected back and recognized. He is taking a sense of a place that is essential but scattered, that is everywhere but hard to see—because you are a part of it, and living it. Instead of palm trees, Irwin is gathering a world that has transitioned over a vast scale of time, manifesting itself through volcanoes and basins and grass and, yes, the ruins of people. As art historian David Raskin wrote, "The aesthetic experience of scale depends on the how successfully artists focus their own values and is a dramatic moment that sometimes endures but for an instant." [2] At Chinati, Irwin's values are simply the values that he was given, and the ultimate value is the sun and light. The sun and the movement of the earth are the oldest things we can see with our eyes. It is weird to feel that. It is weird to know that.

• • •

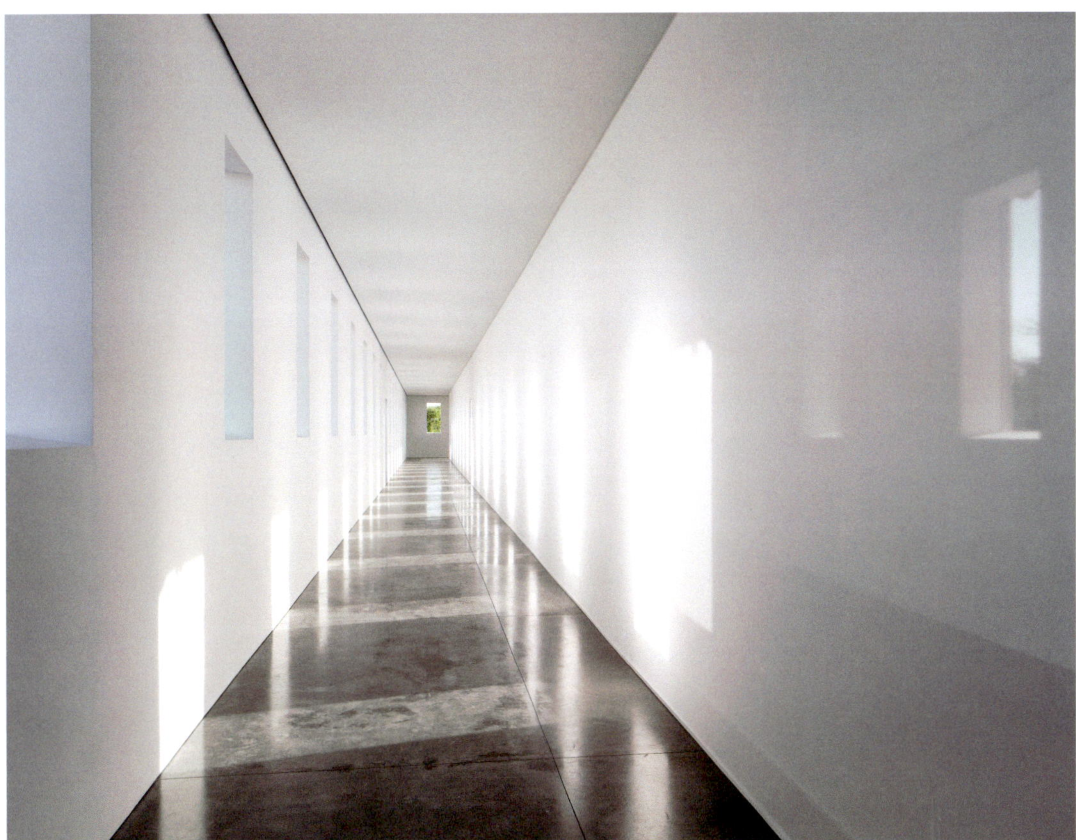

Robert Irwin, *Untitled (dawn to dusk)*, 2016.

When I arrived to see the installation for the first time, Irwin was working on the final details of the installation—one detail in particular. If one looks to the final plans for the building, all of the windows were to be equipped with a series of tints that filtered the sunlight coming in from all sides of the building (plates 47 and 48). It is hard to grasp what the final effect would have been, but I suspect it would have added another dimension to the notion of transition that runs through the entire building, from the dark to light, from solidity to permeability, from east to west. The effect of the light would have probably been pictorial across the surface at dawn and dusk, a series of diminishing rectangles on one side of the building and another series of growing rectangles on the other side, working their way to solid gray or total transparency.

In the end, the decision was made not to add the tints. Thus, the corridors and the south hallway with the scrim doors provide one consistent transition as the sun rises and falls. All at once, the building comes to life in the morning, works to brightness with extinguished shadows at noon, until it eventually finds the moods of the evening. One feels the energy of the sun, how light is both a particle and a wave, at once setting on the surface of the scrims and at other times pushing through and casting its beams on the opposite wall. And if one turns away from the action on the scrims and the play of shapes, looking out the windows on the sides, they are eye level, pitching the eyes upward to the sky with the landscape slightly visible at the bottom. From the light to landscape, or, in Irwin's words: "[T]he view, the landscape outside was like a Dutch painting, just a thin strip of land and the rest all sky."[3]

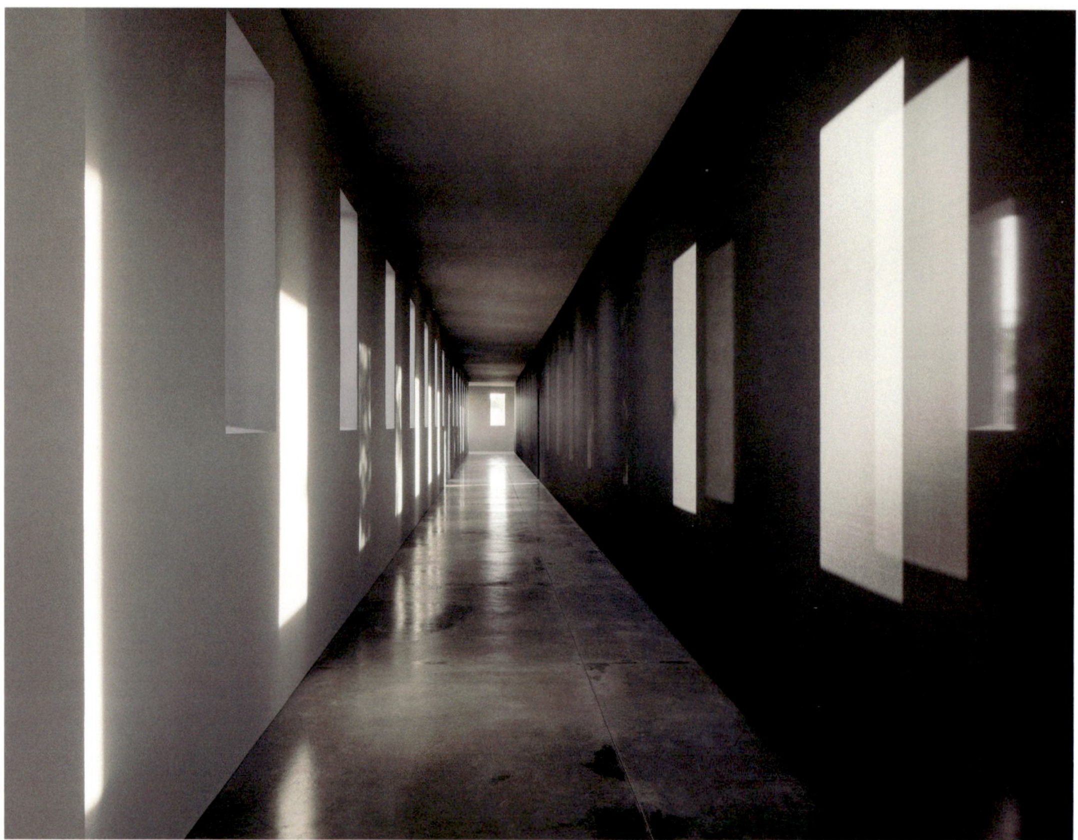

Robert Irwin, *Untitled (dawn to dusk)*, 2016.

I have to admit, when I saw the installation completed and spent some time trying to grapple with the conditions of the site, it was just incredibly pleasant to sit there in the light. On the side with the white scrim, it is such an intense flash of white with a slow dissolve that one remembers that Irwin quote, aptly employed by Matthew Simms in his recent book on Irwin, about what that light can do:

> The sun hits you … and you think, wow, what a wonderful—you know, wow. You know? Then we can start measuring that, and because you're quantifying that and explain why that's a good thing or a bad thing. And we start talking about Vitamin D and we start talking about the sense of wellbeing and all—you know, you play all these games, but finally it's more.[4]

That "more" for me in Marfa in *Untitled (dawn to dusk)* is perhaps a fancy, or perhaps that good-old Vitamin D adding to my well-being, but there was something apt to the point of being a tangible reality that this was once a hospital—that this, for years, saw life and death in transition. Maybe it is that moment in the war movies where the soldier wakes up in a white ward, upon a bed of white sheets, in a corridor fluttering with nurses in white, alive.

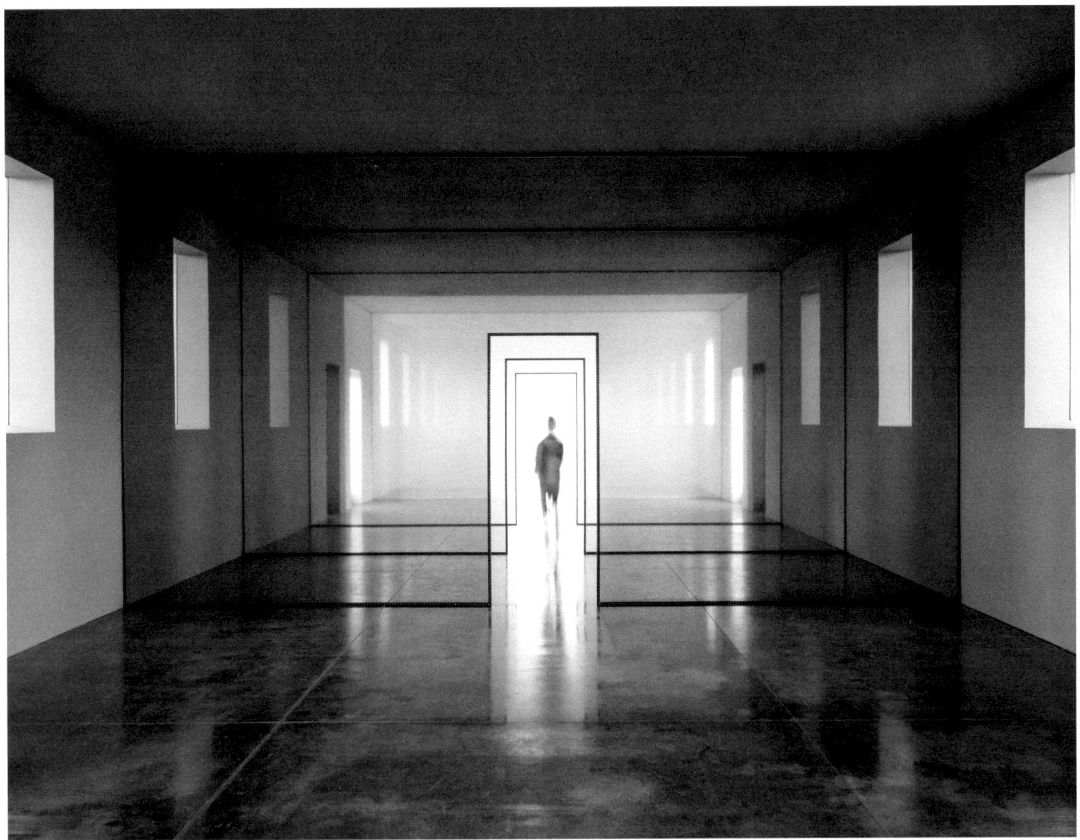

Robert Irwin, *Untitled (dawn to dusk)*, 2016.

Notes

1 Robert Irwin, quoted in Michael Agresta, "Miracle in the Desert," *Texas Monthly*, July, 2016, http://www.texasmonthly.com/the-culture/robert-irwin-installation-chinati-marfa/.
2 David Raskin, "Shapiro's Degrees of Scale" in *Joel Shapiro*, exh. cat. (New York and London: Dominique Lévy, 2012), 61.
3 Irwin, quoted in a 2012 interview posted on the Chinati website, n.d., https://chinati.org/robertirwin/irwin-at-chinati.
4 Matthew Simms, *Robert Irwin: A Conditional Art* (New Haven, CT and London: Yale University Press, 2016), 315.

EXHIBITION CHECKLIST

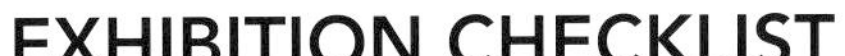

Cal State Long Beach Window Wall, 1975–76
ink, pencil, and marker on paper
Sheet: 23 x 31 1/4 inches (58.4 x 79.4 cm)
Collection of the University Art Museum, California State University, Long Beach

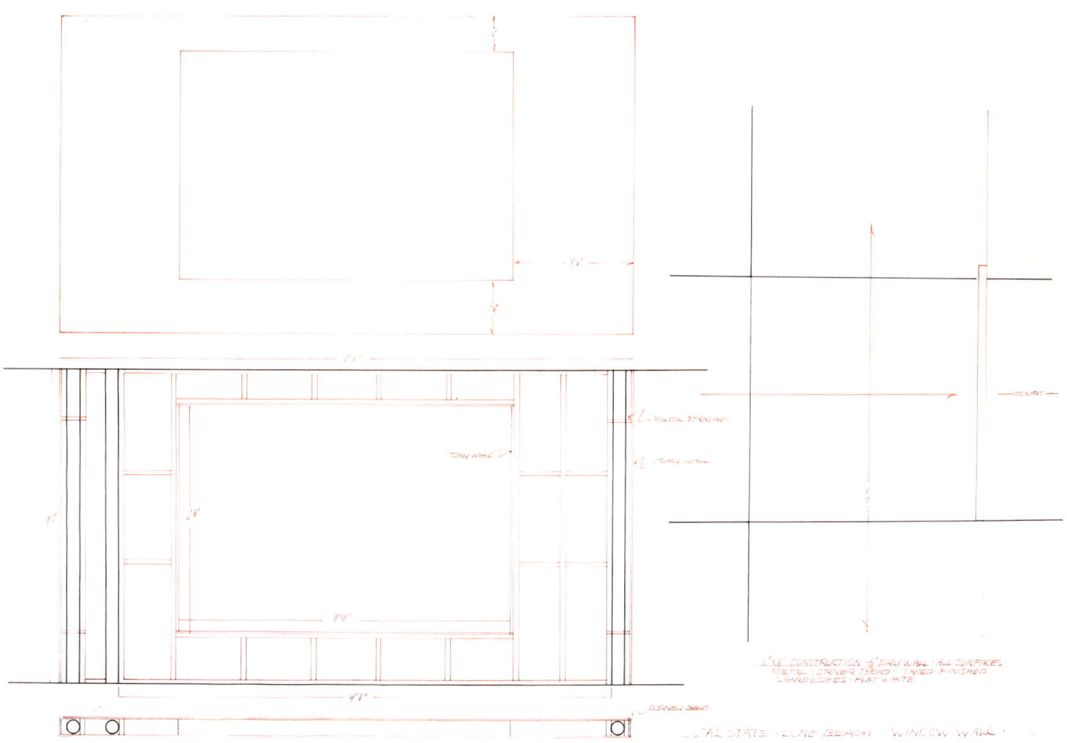

Tilted Planes, proposed 1978 (unrealized), Oval Mall, Ohio State University, Columbus, 1978
graphite and color pencil on vellum
Sheet: 20 x 37 inches (50.8 x 94 cm)
Collection of the Palm Springs Art Museum, Gift of L.J. Cella

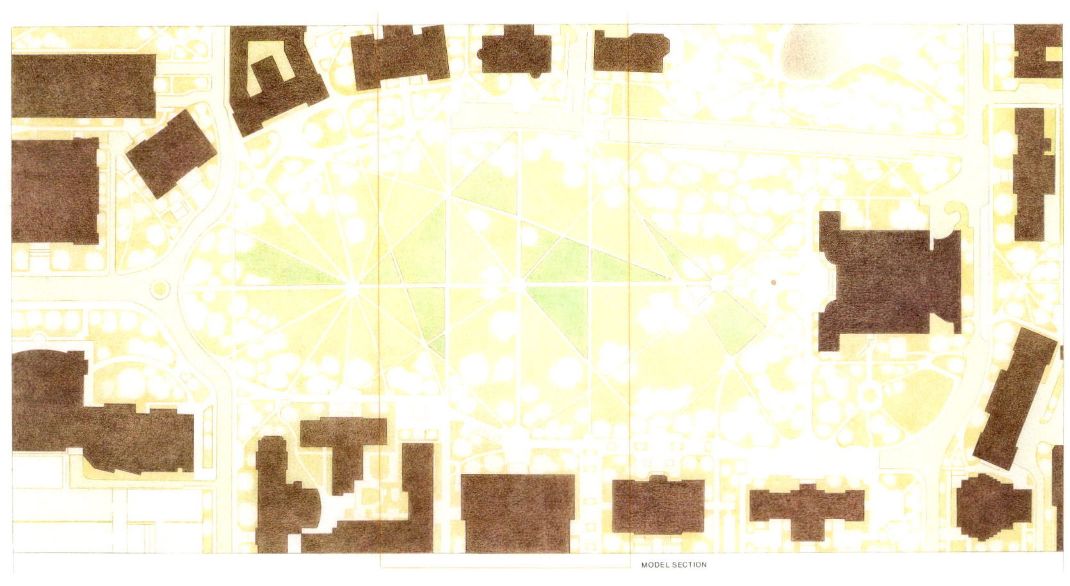

MODEL SECTION

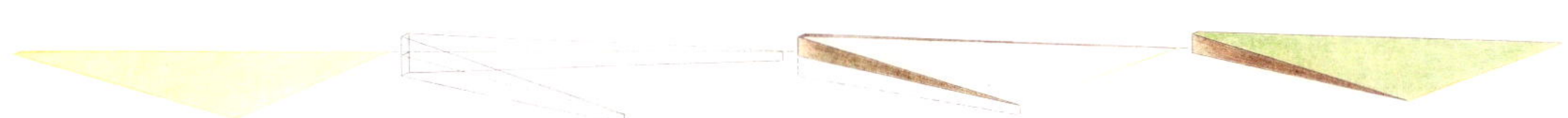

Tilted Planes, proposed 1978 (unrealized), Oval Mall, Ohio State University, Columbus, 1978
mixed media model
7 1/4 x 25 1/2 x 45 1/4 inches (18.4 x 64.8 x 114.9 cm)
Collection Museum of Contemporary Art San Diego
Museum purchase with proceeds from Museum of Contemporary Art San Diego
Art Auction 2006, 2006.49

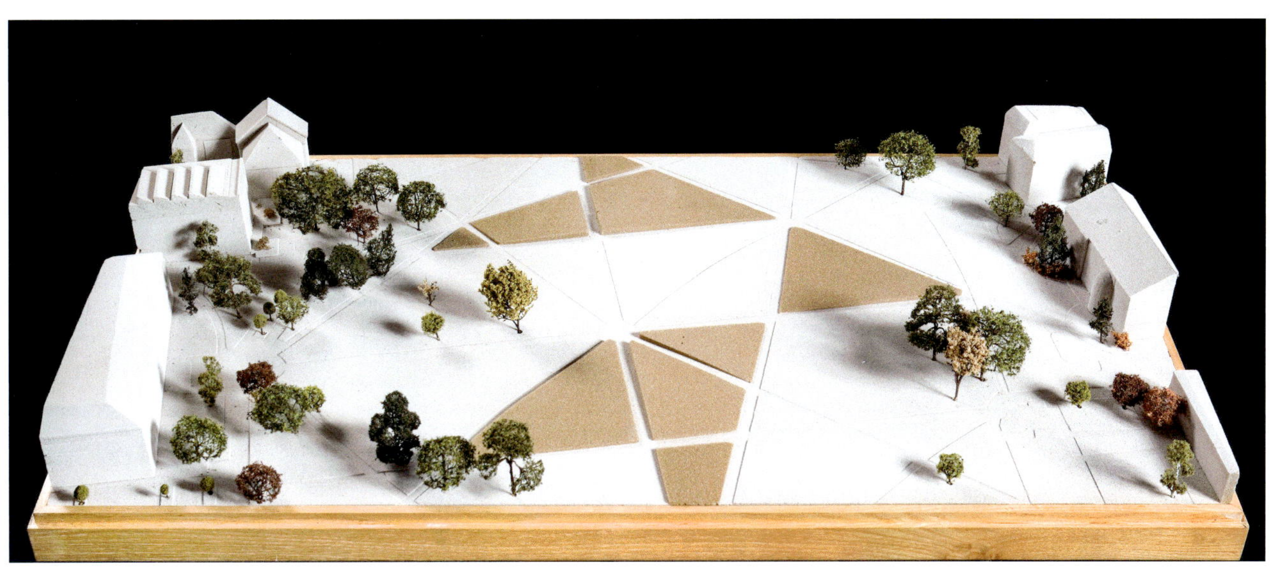

Plate 4

Two Running Violet V Forms, 1982
ink and pencil on paper
24 x 46 inches (61 x 116.8 cm)
Stuart Collection Records, Special Collections & Archives, University of California, San Diego

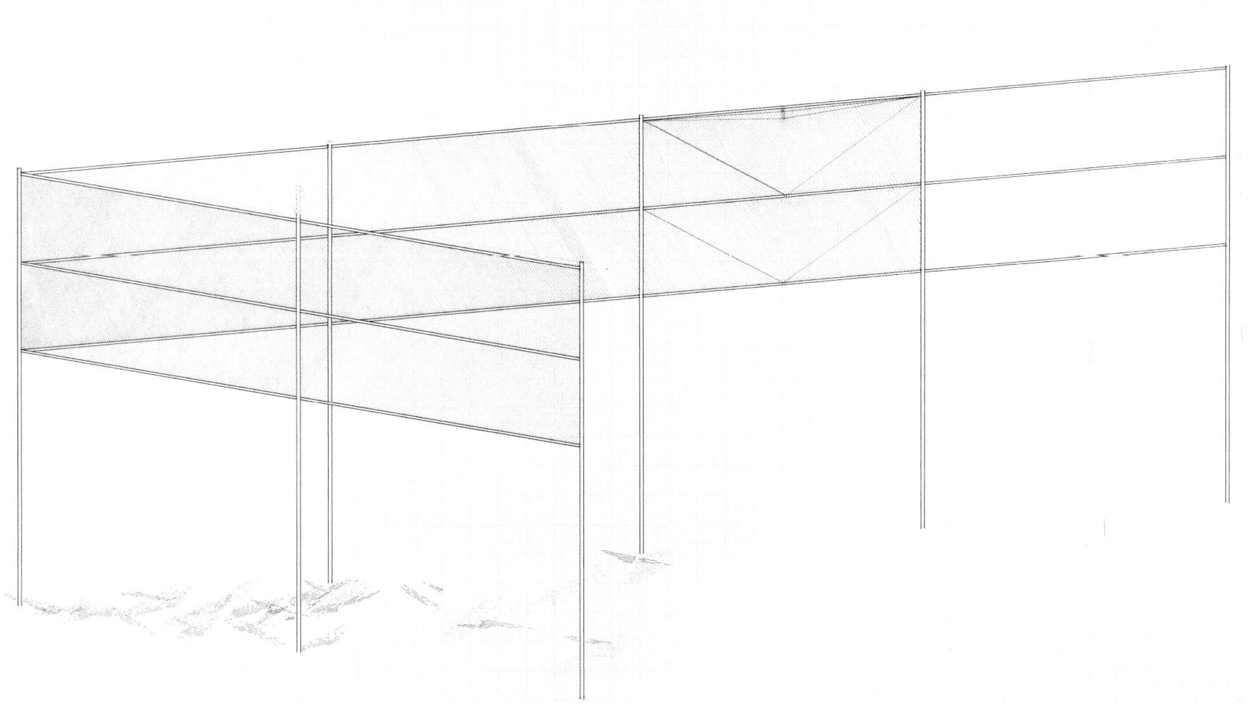

Plate 5

Three Primary Forms (Battery Park City World Financial Center) (unrealized), 1983
color pencil on paper
67 x 61 inches (170.2 x 154.9 cm)
Collection Museum of Contemporary Art San Diego
Gift of Arne and Milly Glimcher, 2007.61

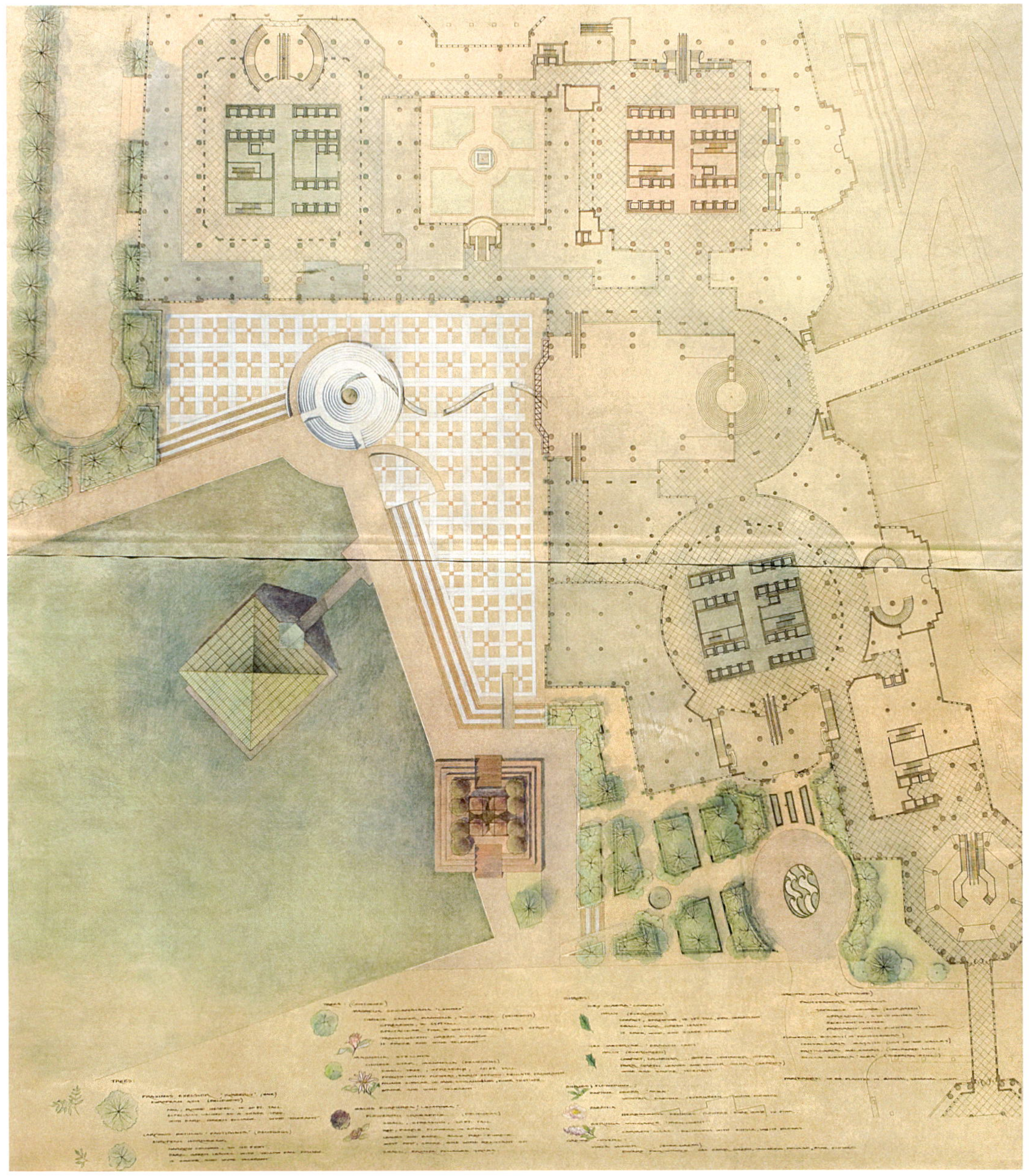

*Arts Enrichment Master Plan, proposed 1986 (unrealized),
Miami International Airport, Episodic Flow Chart (First Presentation)*, 1986
ink drawing on vellum with watercolor transfer tape
Sheet: 29 1/4 x 46 3/4 inches (74.3 x 118.7 cm)
Framed: 39 x 67 x 3 inches (99.1 x 170.2 x 7.6 cm)
Collection Museum of Contemporary Art San Diego
Promised gift of L.J. Cella

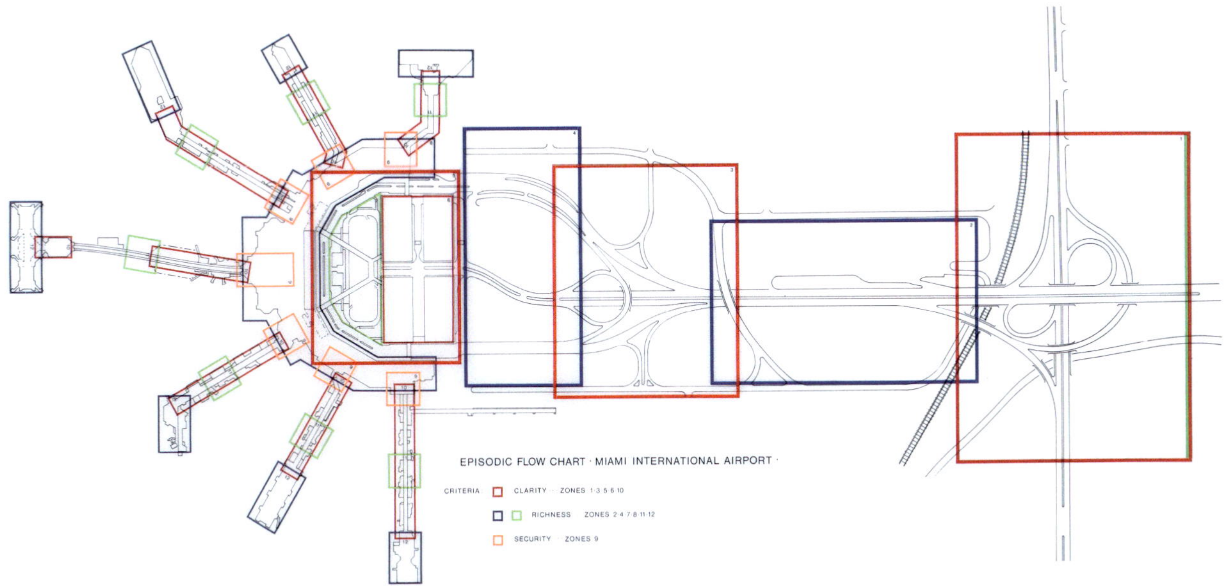

EPISODIC FLOW CHART · MIAMI INTERNATIONAL AIRPORT ·
CRITERIA
CLARITY · ZONES 1·3·5·6·10
RICHNESS ZONES 2·4·7·8·11·12
SECURITY · ZONES 9

Arts Enrichment Master Plan, proposed 1986 (unrealized)
Miami International Airport Master Plan (First Presentation), 1986
color pencil on vellum
Sheet: 38 1/4 x 56 inches (97.2 x 142.2 cm)
Framed: 38 1/2 x 56 1/4 x 2 inches (97.8 x 142.9 x 5.1 cm)
Collection Museum of Contemporary Art San Diego
Museum purchase with Jackie and Rea Axline Funds, 2004.41

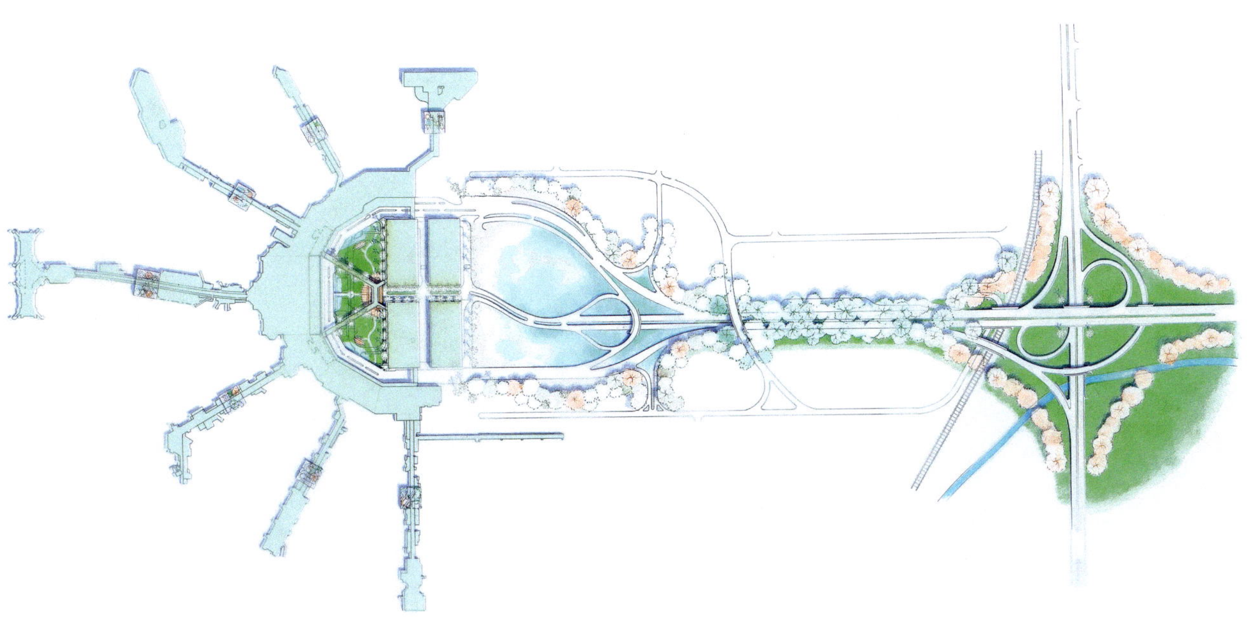

Arts Enrichment Master Plan, proposed 1986 (unrealized),
Miami International Airport Terminal (First Presentation), 1986
color pencil on vellum
Sheet: 38 3/8 x 56 7/16 inches (97.5 x 143.4 cm)
Framed: 39 x 67 x 3 inches (99.1 x 170.2 x 7.6 cm)
Collection Museum of Contemporary Art San Diego
Promised gift of L.J. Cella

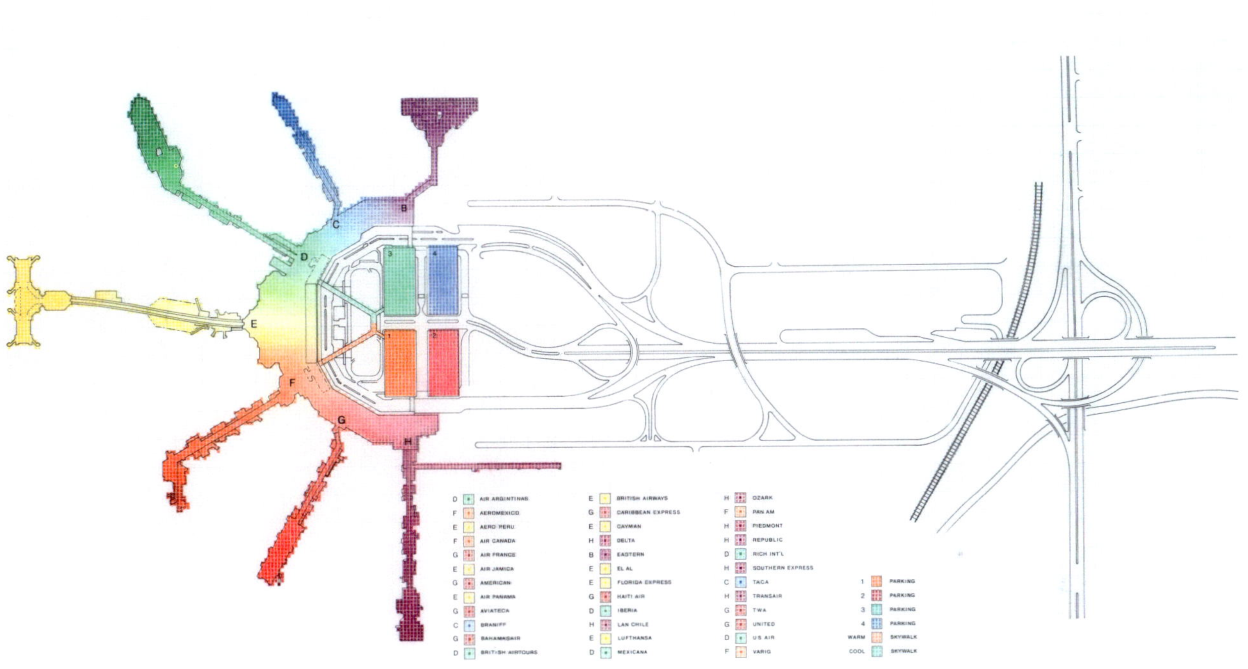

D AIR ARGINTINAS
F AEROMEXICO
E AERO PERU
F AIR CANADA
G AIR FRANCE
E AIR JAMICA
G AMERICAN
E AIR PANAMA
G AVIATECA
C BRANIFF
G BAHAMASAIR
D BRITISH AIRTOURS
E BRITISH AIRWAYS
G CARIBBEAN EXPRESS
E CAYMAN
H DELTA
B EASTERN
E EL AL
E FLORIDA EXPRESS
G HAITI AIR
D IBERIA
H LAN CHILE
E LUFTHANSA
D MEXICANA
H OZARK
F PAN AM
H PIEDMONT
H REPUBLIC
D RICH INT'L
H SOUTHERN EXPRESS
C TACA
H TRANSAIR
G TWA
G UNITED
D US AIR
F VARIG
1 PARKING
2 PARKING
3 PARKING
4 PARKING
WARM SKYWALK
COOL SKYWALK

Plate 9

Arts Enrichment Master Plan, proposed 1986 (unrealized)
Miami International Airport Toll Plaza (Third Presentation), 1986
color ink on paper (two views)
44 x 58 inches (111.8 x 147.3 cm)
Collection Museum of Contemporary Art San Diego
Museum purchase with Jackie and Rea Axline Funds, 2004.45

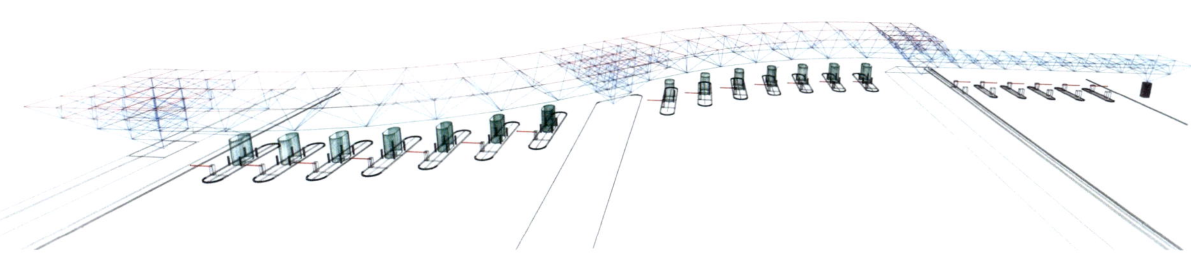

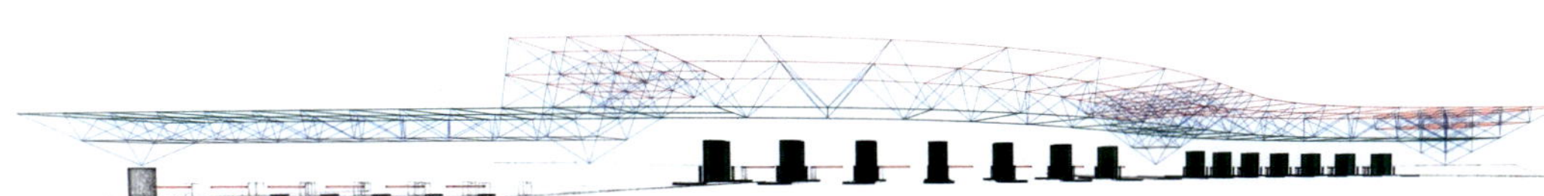

Plate 10

Arts Enrichment Master Plan, proposed 1986 (unrealized),
Miami International Airport Toll Plaza Landscape Plan, Third Presentation, 1986
color pencil on vellum
Sheet: 34 1/4 x 48 inches (87 x 121.9 cm)
Framed: 44 x 58 x 2 inches (111.8 x 147.3 x 5.1 cm)
Collection Museum of Contemporary Art San Diego
Promised gift of L.J. Cella

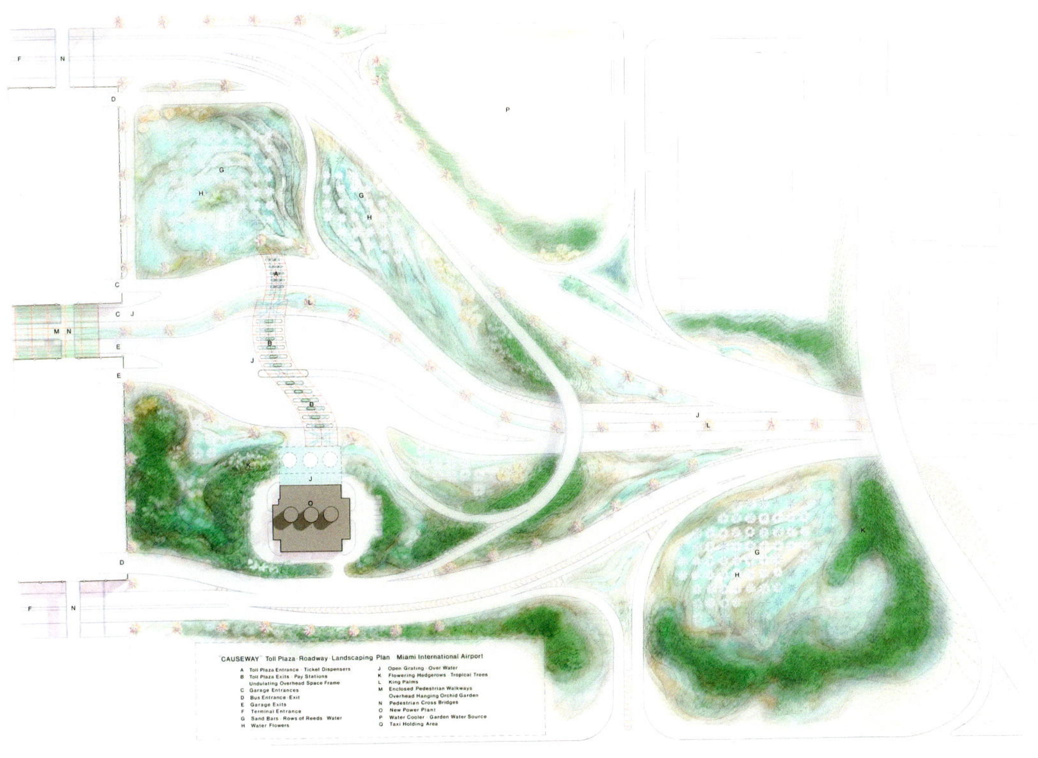

"CAUSEWAY" Toll Plaza·Roadway·Landscaping Plan   Miami International Airport
A   Toll Plaza Entrance · Ticket Dispensers
B   Toll Plaza Exits · Pay Stations
     Undulating Overhead Space Frame
C   Garage Entrances
D   Bus Entrance·Exit
E   Garage Exits
F   Terminal Entrance
G   Sand Bars · Rows of Reeds · Water
H   Water Flowers
J   Open Grating · Over Water
K   Flowering Hedgerows · Tropical Trees
L   King Palms
M   Enclosed Pedestrian Walkways
     Overhead Hanging Orchid Garden
N   Pedestrian Cross Bridges
O   New Power Plant
P   Water Cooler · Garden Water Source
Q   Taxi Holding Area

Arts Enrichment Master Plan, proposed 1986 (unrealized),
Miami International Airport, Central Park Plan Plant Materials, 1986
photographic collage
Sheet: 41 1/4 x 39 1/2 inches (104.8 x 100.3 cm)
Framed: 43 x 42 x 2 inches (109.2 x 106.7 x 5.1 cm)
Collection Museum of Contemporary Art San Diego
Promised gift of L.J. Cella

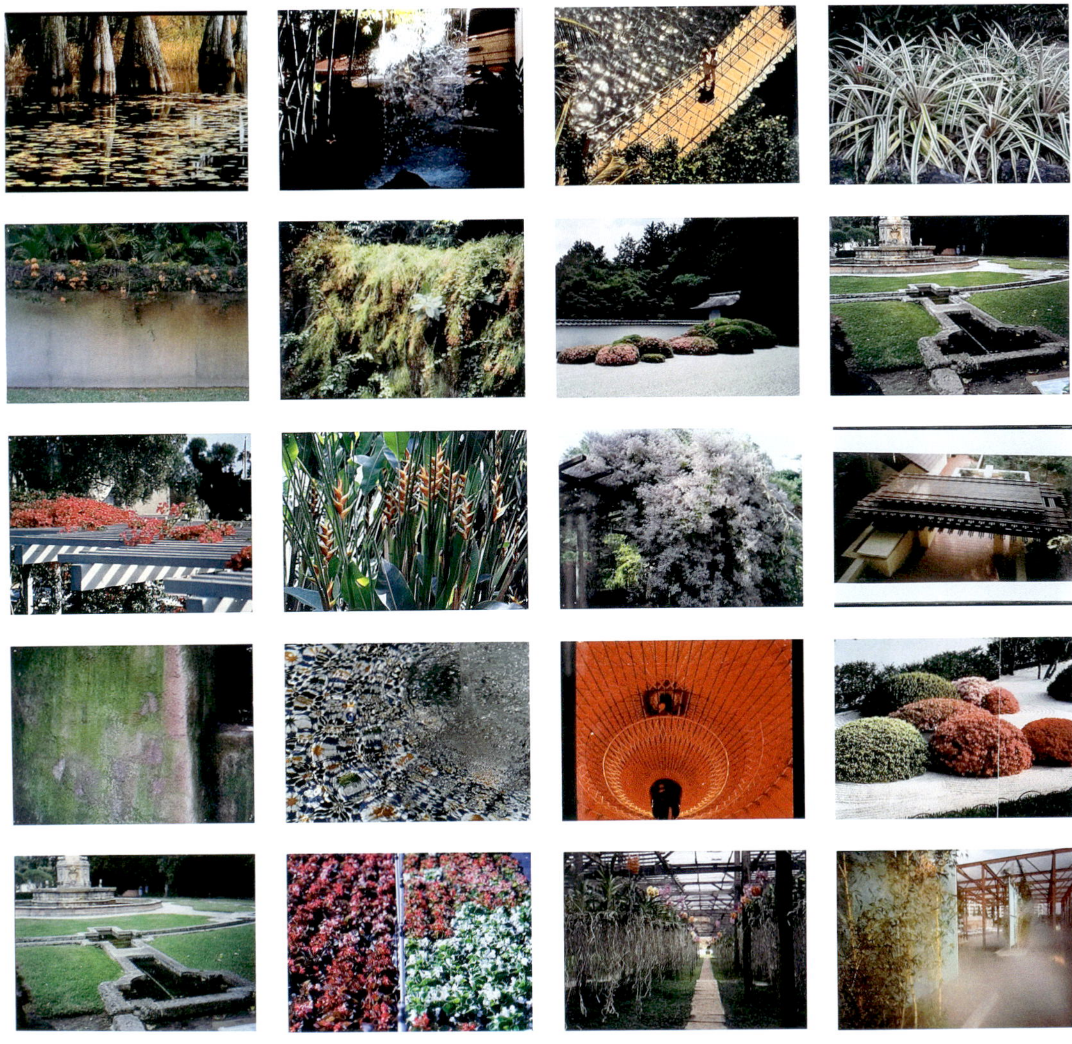

Arts Enrichment Master Plan, proposed 1986 (unrealized),
Miami International Airport, Toll Plaza Plant Materials, 1986
photographic collage
Sheet: 41 1/4 x 39 1/2 inches (104.8 x 100.3 cm)
Framed: 42 x 39 x 2 inches (106.7 x 99.1 x 5.1 cm)
Collection Museum of Contemporary Art San Diego
Promised gift of L.J. Cella

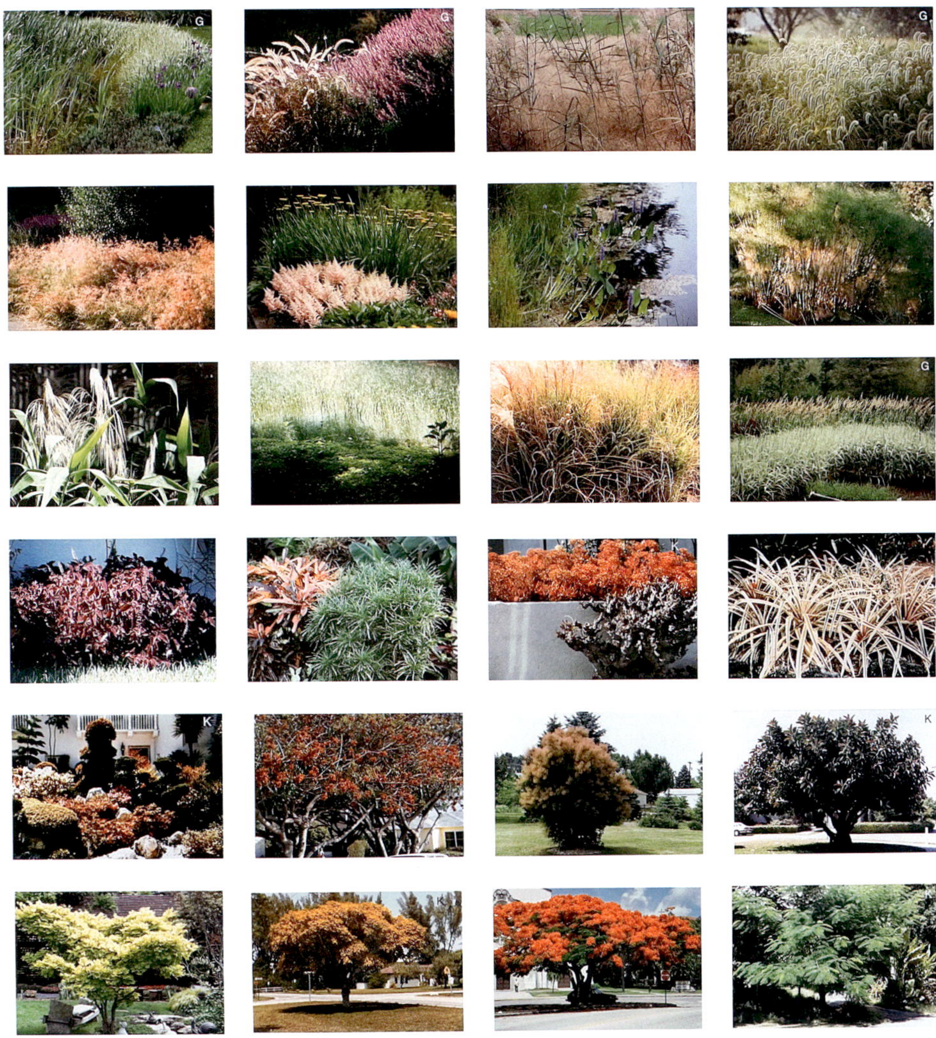

Arts Enrichment Master Plan, proposed 1986 (unrealized),
Miami International Airport, Central Park, Second Presentation, 1986
photo composite with drawings and watercolor transfer tape
Sheet: 37 1/4 x 81 inches (94.6 x 205.7 cm)
Framed: 38 x 84 x 3 inches (96.5 x 213.4 x 7.6 cm)
Collection Museum of Contemporary Art San Diego
Promised gift of L.J. Cella

CENTRAL PARK

PRINCIPAL STRATEGY
heighten awareness

PRIMARY METHODS
raise sensory threshold
create options
clear sense of place
perceptual play

ROBERT IRWIN

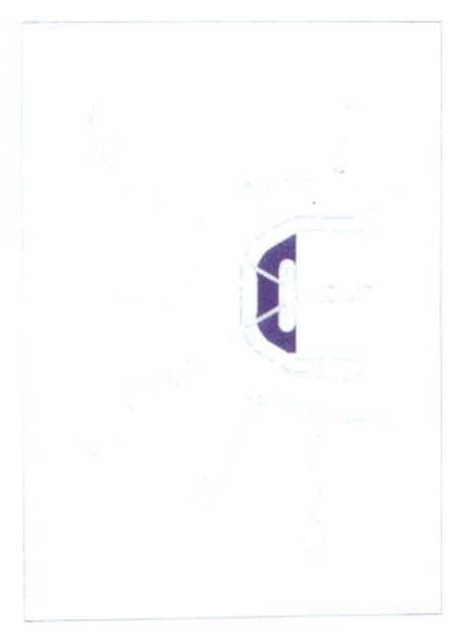

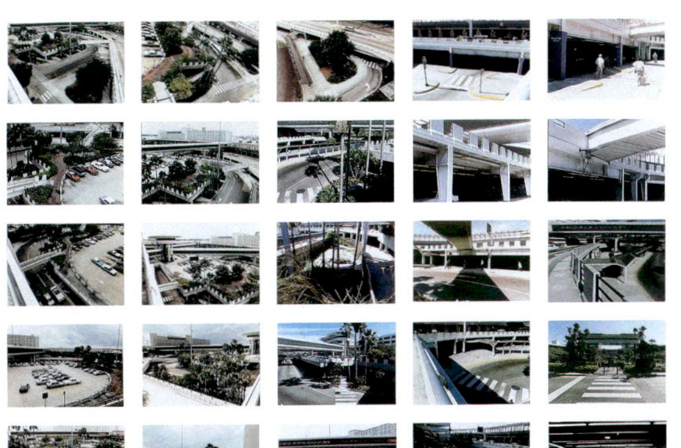

87

Arts Enrichment Master Plan, proposed 1986 (unrealized),
Miami International Airport (First Presentation), 1986
color pencil on vellum
Sheet: 29 x 32 1/4 inches (73.7 x 81.9 cm)
Framed: 39 x 42 x 2 inches (99.1 x 106.7 x 5.1 cm)
Collection Museum of Contemporary Art San Diego
Promised gift of L.J. Cella

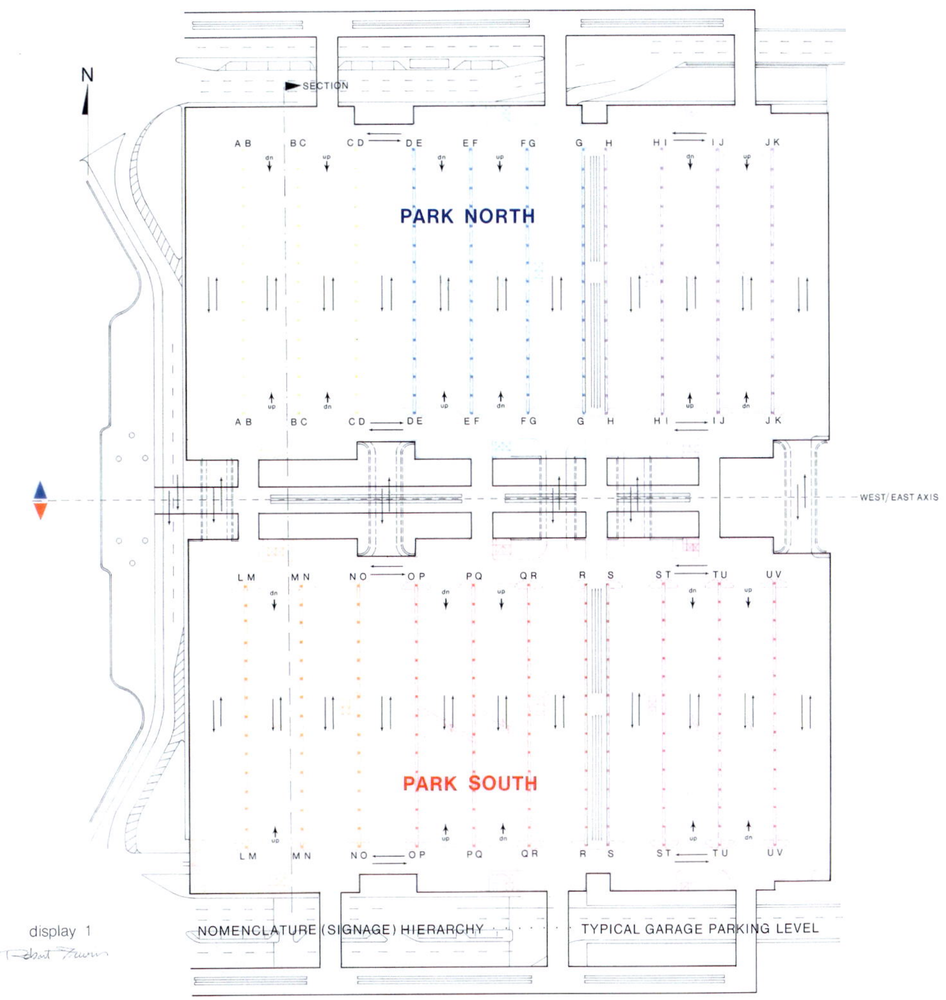

display 1

NOMENCLATURE (SIGNAGE) HIERARCHY · · · · · · TYPICAL GARAGE PARKING LEVEL

Plate 15

Arts Enrichment Master Plan, proposed 1986 (unrealized),
Miami International Airport, Central Park Plan View (Third Presentation), 1986
color pencil and ink on vellum
Sheet: 28 3/4 x 56 inches (73 x 142.2 cm)
Framed: 39 x 67 x 3 inches (99.1 x 170.2 x 7.6 cm)
Collection Museum of Contemporary Art San Diego
Promised gift of L.J. Cella

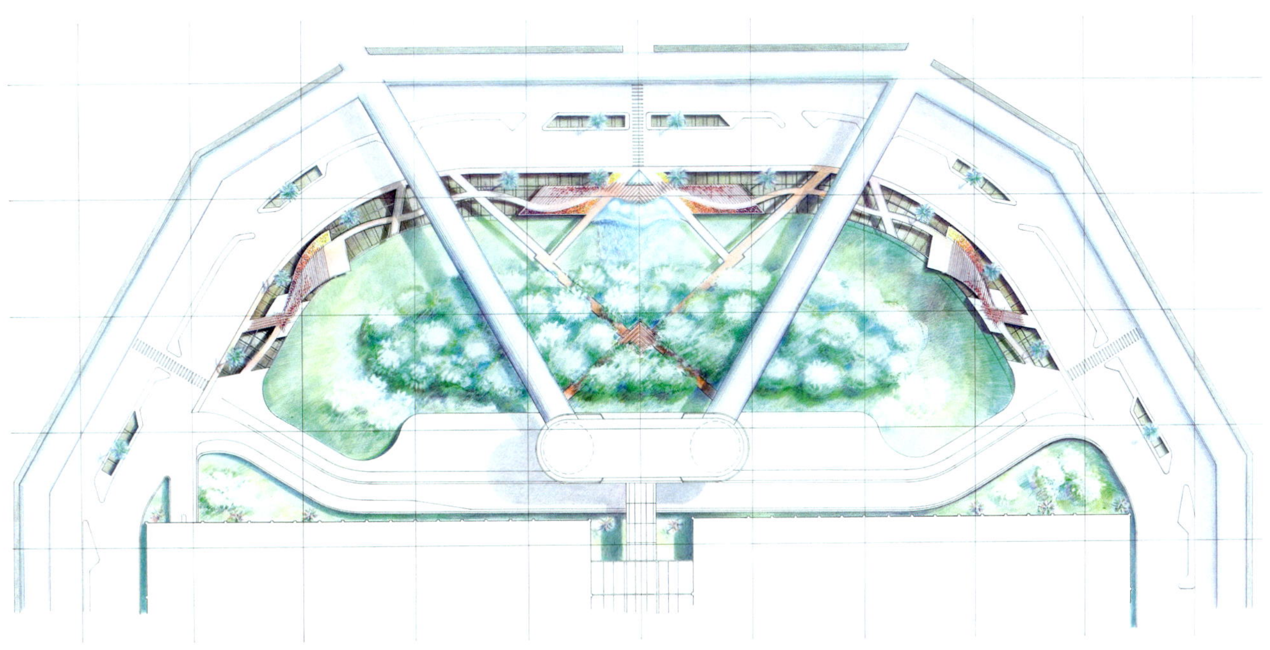

Plate 16

Two Architectural Towers, proposed 1989 (unrealized), City Front Plaza,
Chicago: Chicago Tower 1900, 1989
mixed media model
55 3/4 x 21 3/8 x 21 3/8 inches (141.6 x 54.3 x 54.3 cm)
Collection Museum of Contemporary Art San Diego
Museum purchase with Jackie and Rea Axline Funds, 2004.46.a-d

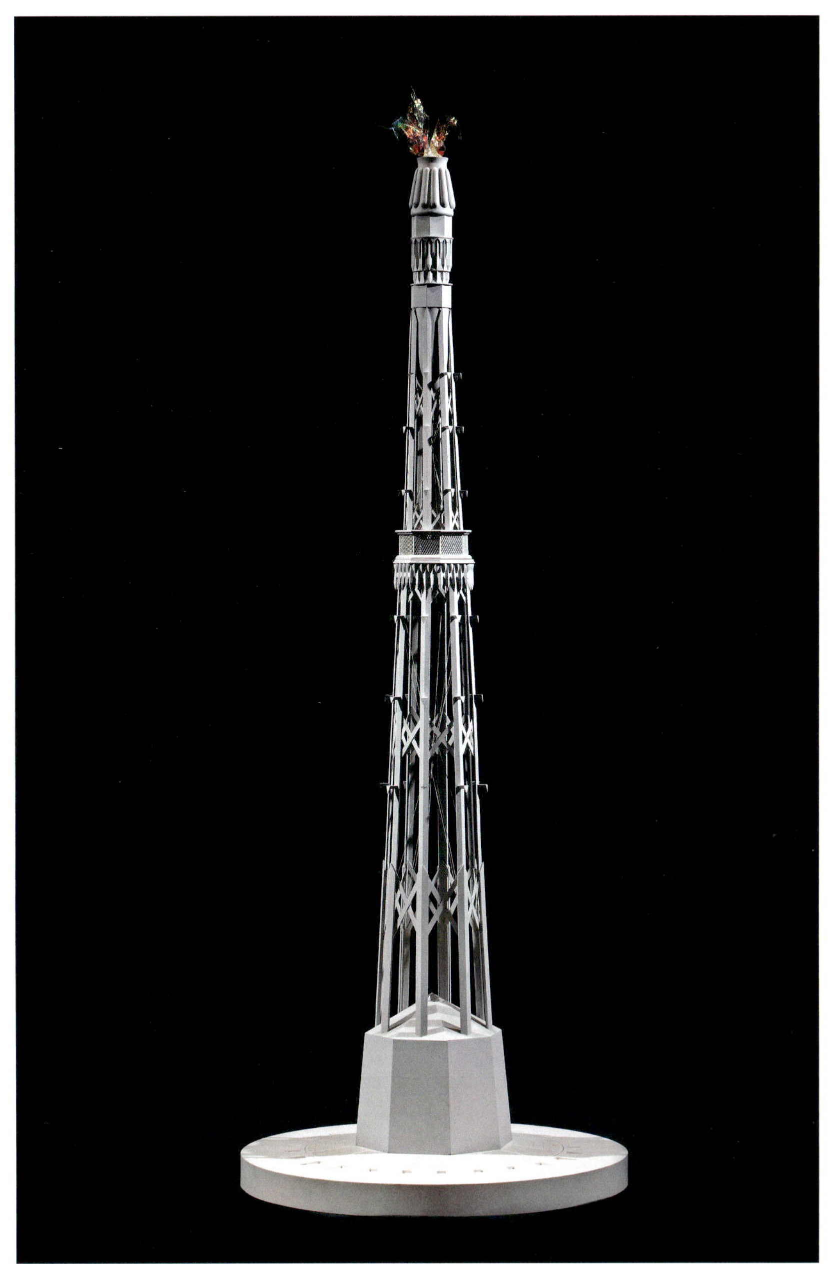

Plate 17

Two Architectural Towers, proposed 1989 (unrealized), City Front Plaza,
Chicago: Chicago Tower 1930, 1989
mixed media model
46 5/8 x 8 1/8 x 8 inches (118.4 x 20.6 x 20.3 cm)
Collection Museum of Contemporary Art San Diego
Museum purchase with Jackie and Rea Axline Funds, 2004.47.a-d

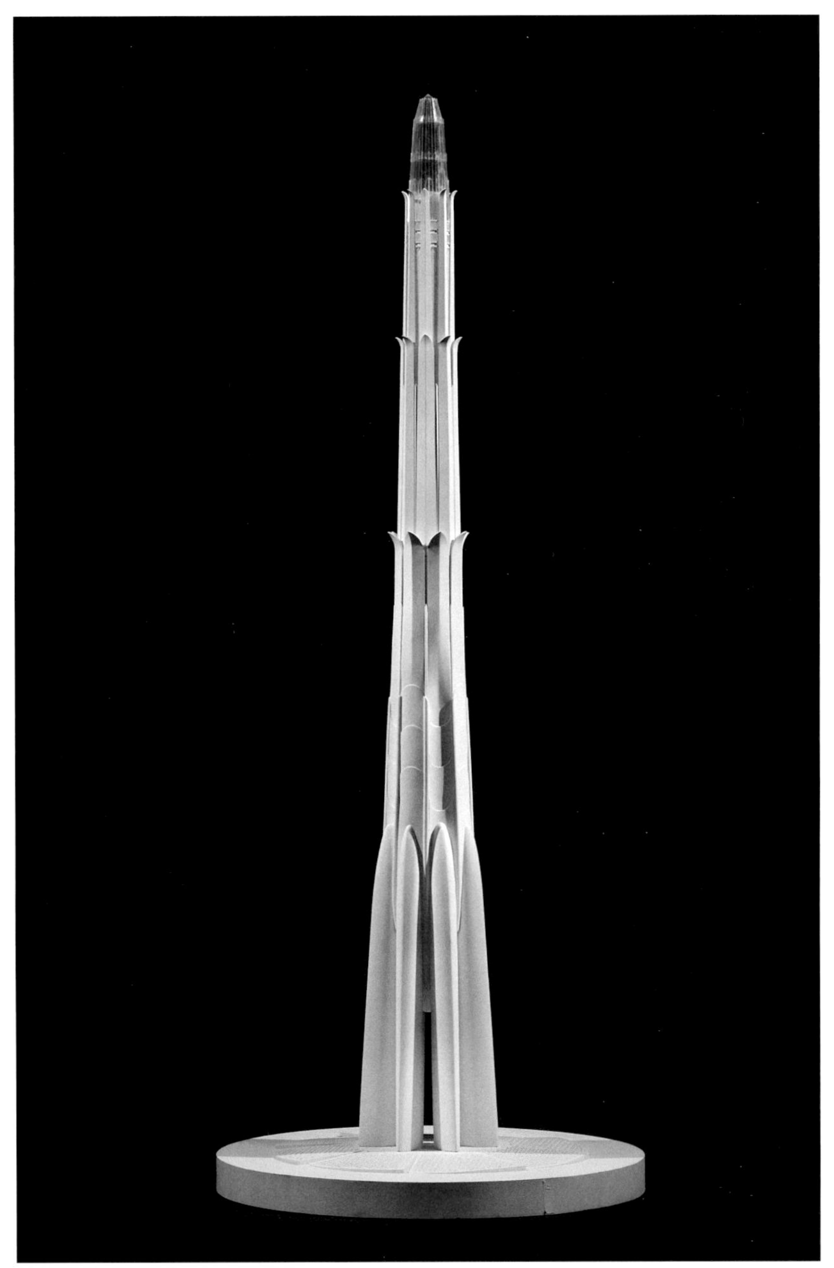

Getty Center Central Garden, Preliminary Plan (August 1993), presentation drawing, 1993
pen on paper
Drawing: 59 ½ x 35 ½ inches (151.13 x 90.17 cm)
Institutional Archives, Getty Research Institute, Los Angeles (1998.IA.15)

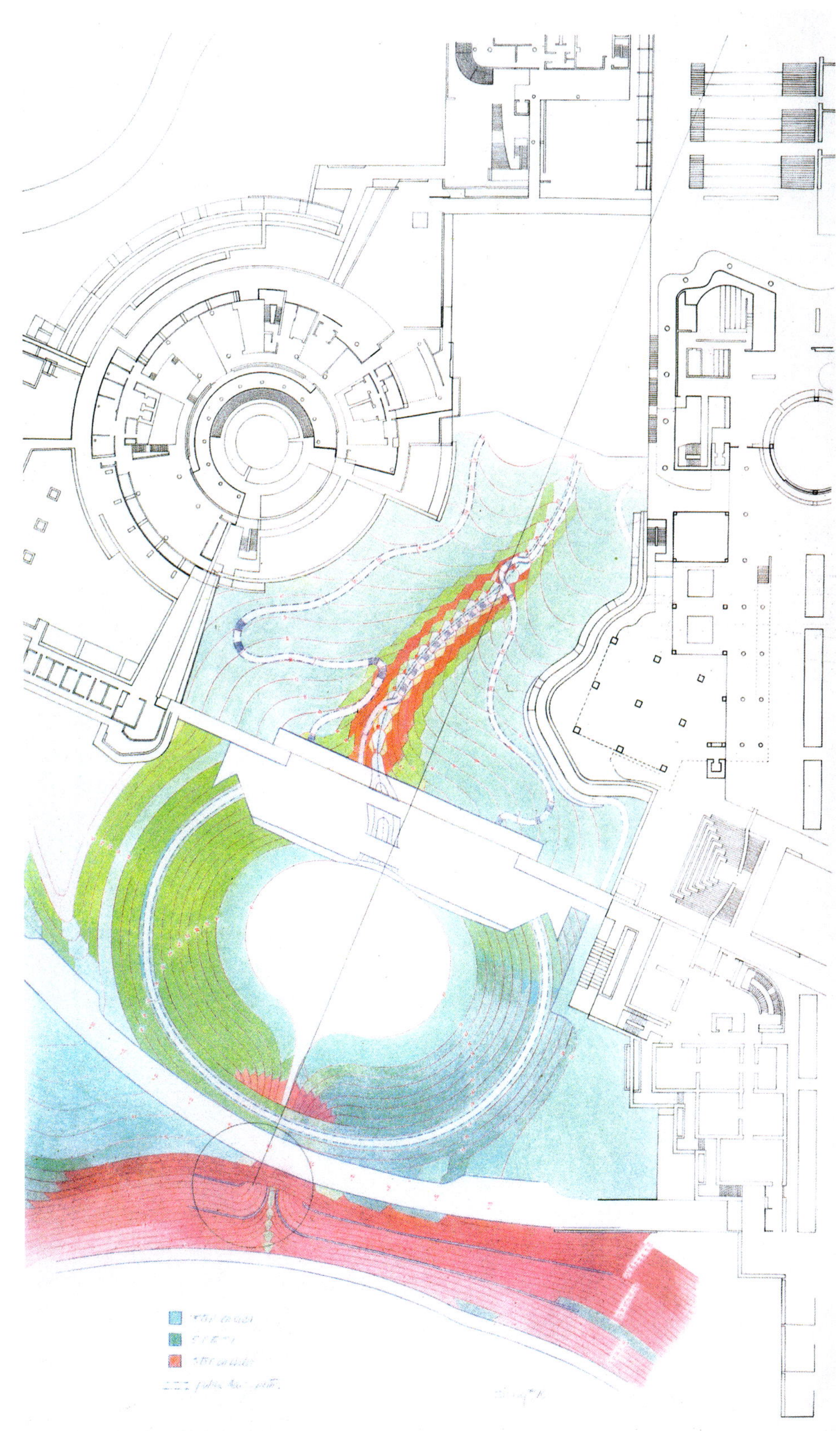

Getty Center Central Garden, Preliminary Plan (March 1994), 1994
pen on paper
Drawing: 60 ¼ x 35 ½" (153.04 x 90.17 cm)
Institutional Archives, Getty Research Institute, Los Angeles (1998.IA.15)

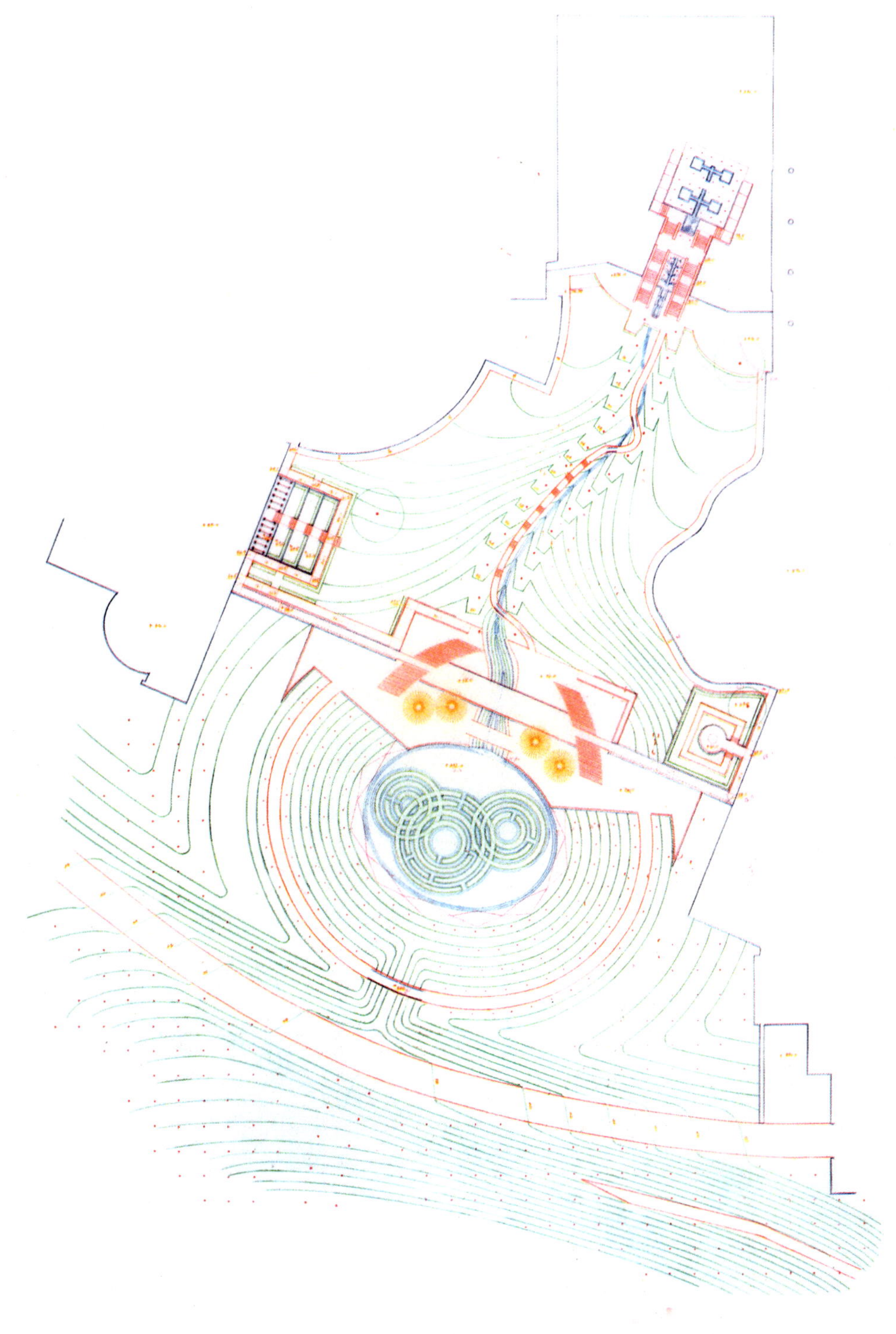

Plate 20

Getty Central Garden Railing, 1994
wood model
8 1/2 x 31 1/2 inches (21.6 x 80 cm)
Collection of the Artist

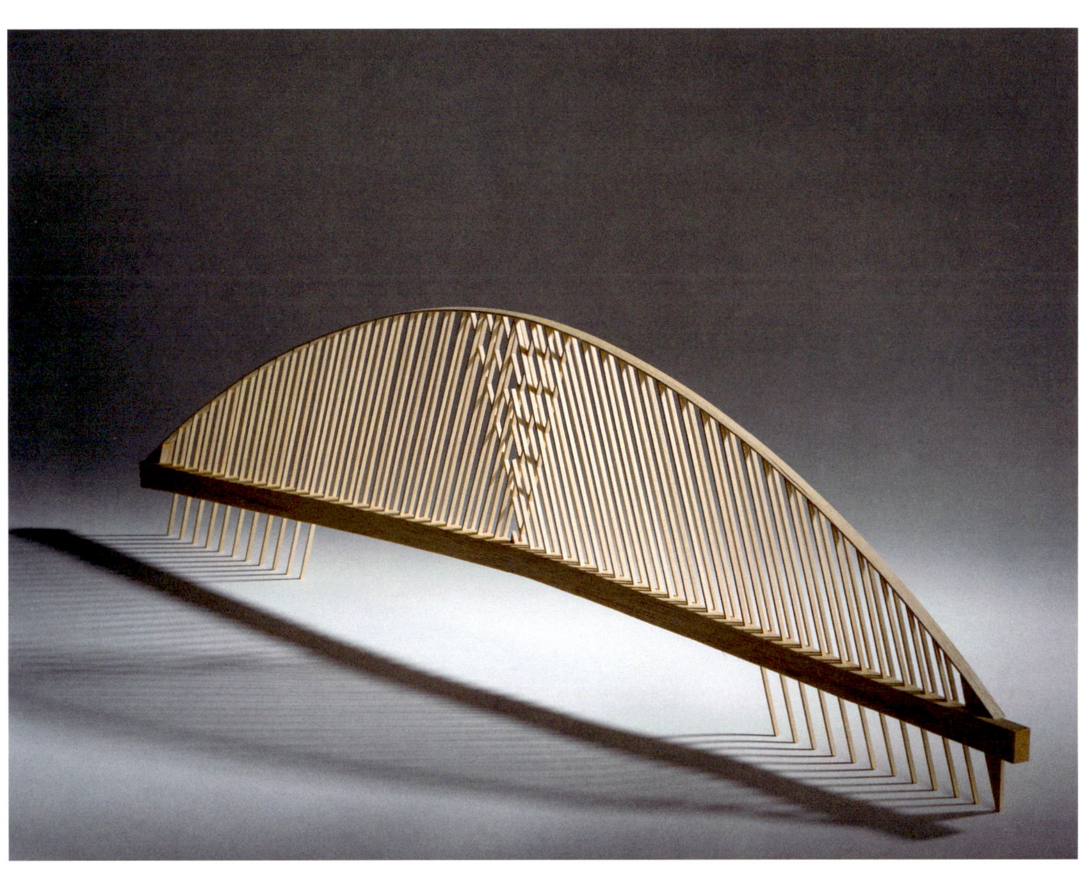

Plate 21

Getty Center Central Garden, detail of Terrace Garden, ca. 1995
color pencil on Mylar
22 x 44 inches (55.9 x 111.8 cm)
Getty Research Institute, Los Angeles (940081), roll T21

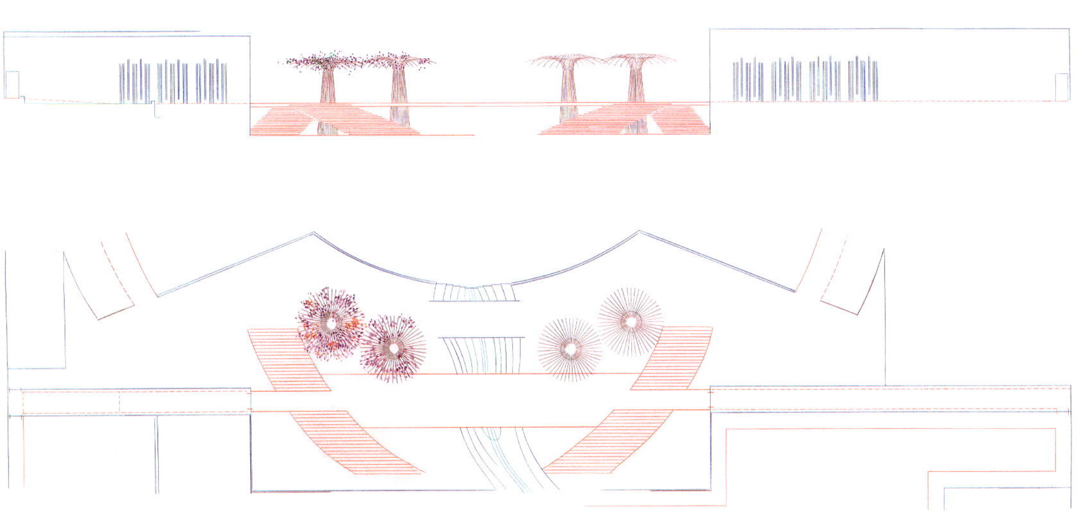

Plate 22

Getty Center Central Garden, Bougainvillea Arbors, ca. 1995
color pencil and felt tip pen on Mylar
50 x 30 inches (127 x 76.2 cm)
Getty Research Institute, Los Angeles (940081), roll T21

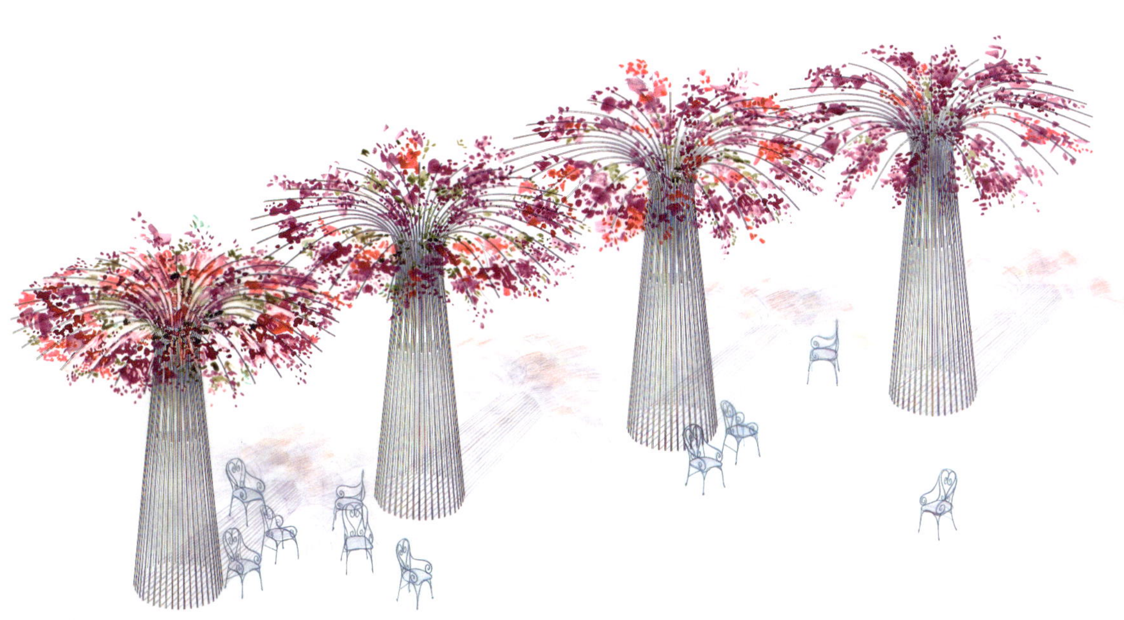

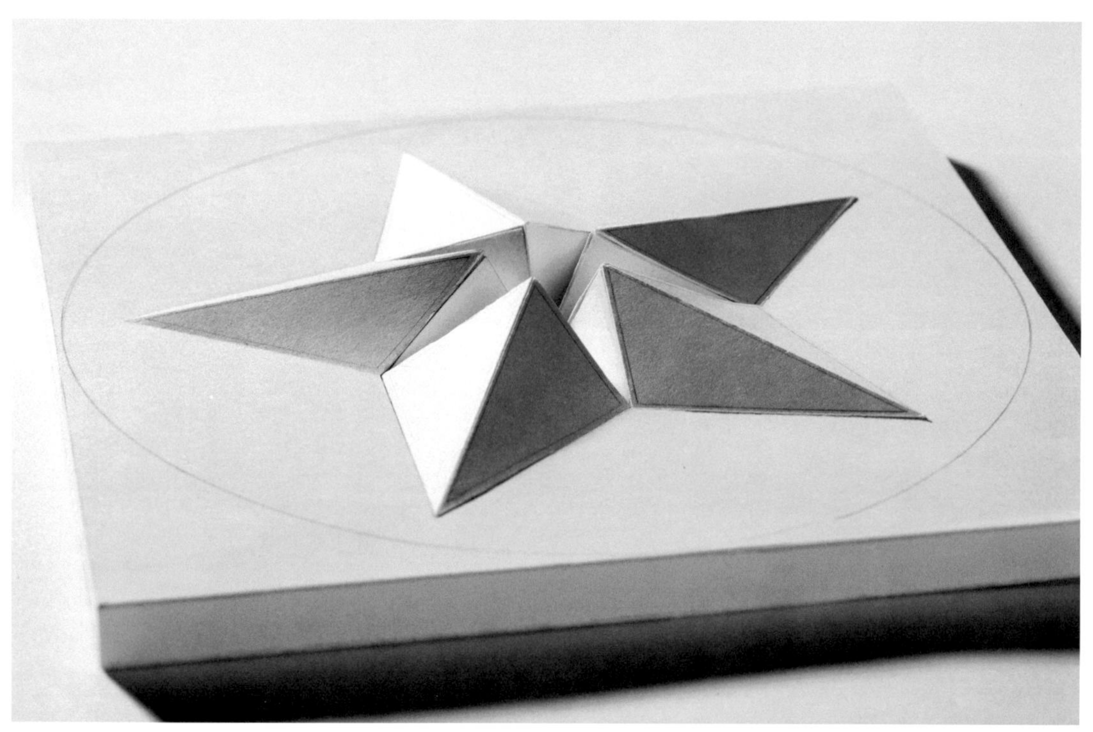

Plate 23

Fortune Teller, ca. 1998
cardboard model
1 x 6 x 6 inches (2.5 x 15.2 x 15.2 cm)
Collection of the Artist

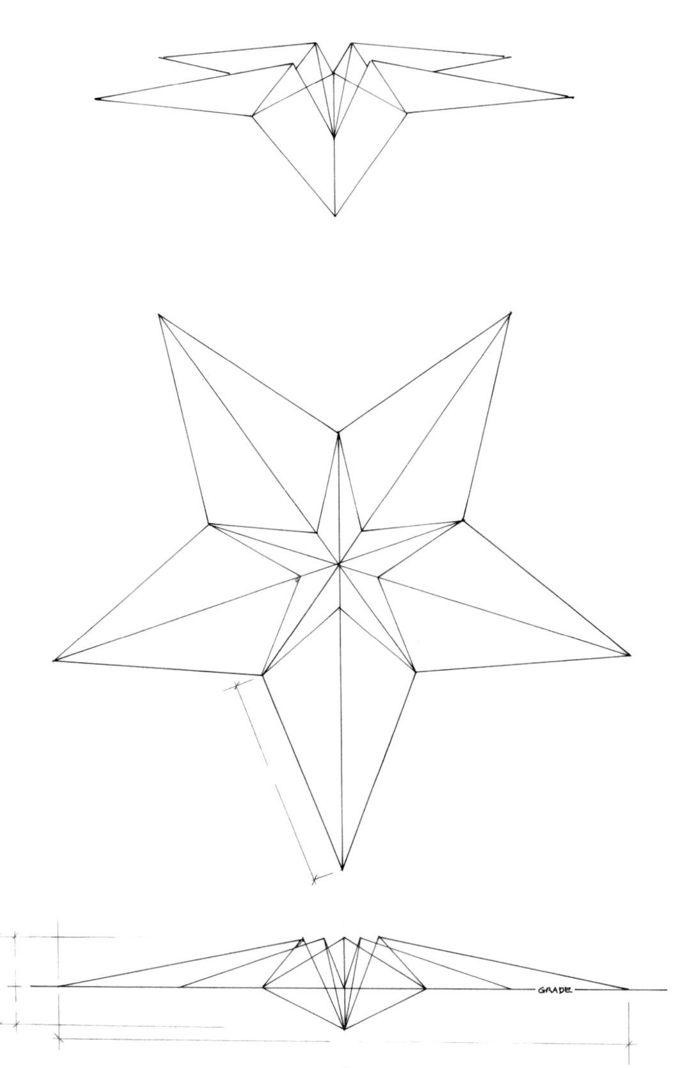

Plate 24

Fortune Teller, ca. 1998
graphite on vellum
Composition: 18 x 11 inches (45.7 x 27.9 cm)
Collection Museum of Contemporary Art San Diego
Promised gift of L.J. Cella

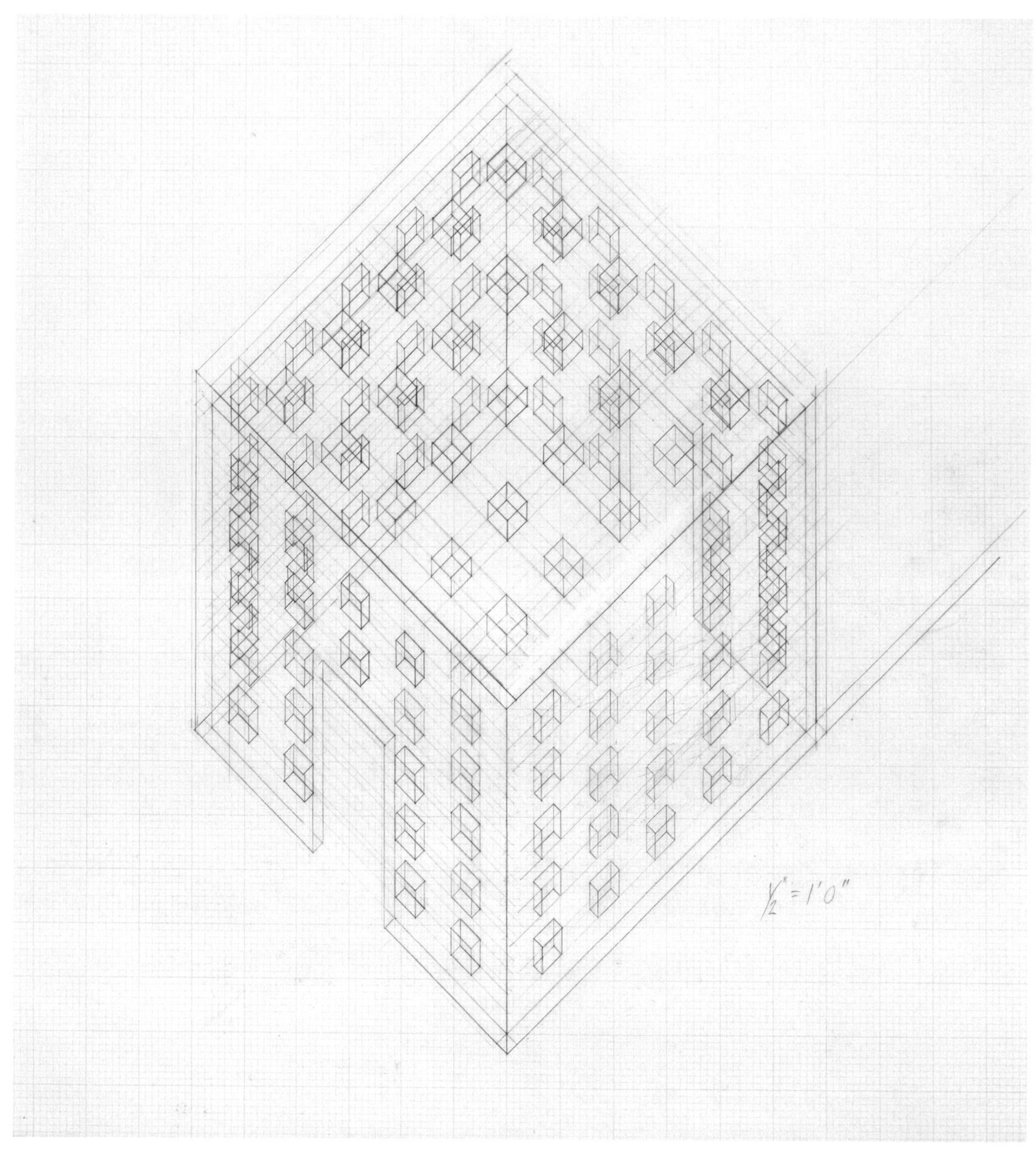

Plate 25

Cyclops House (closed pattern), ca. 1998
color pencil and graphite on graph paper
Composition: 21 x 24 inches (53.3 x 61 cm)
Collection Museum of Contemporary Art San Diego
Promised gift of L.J. Cella

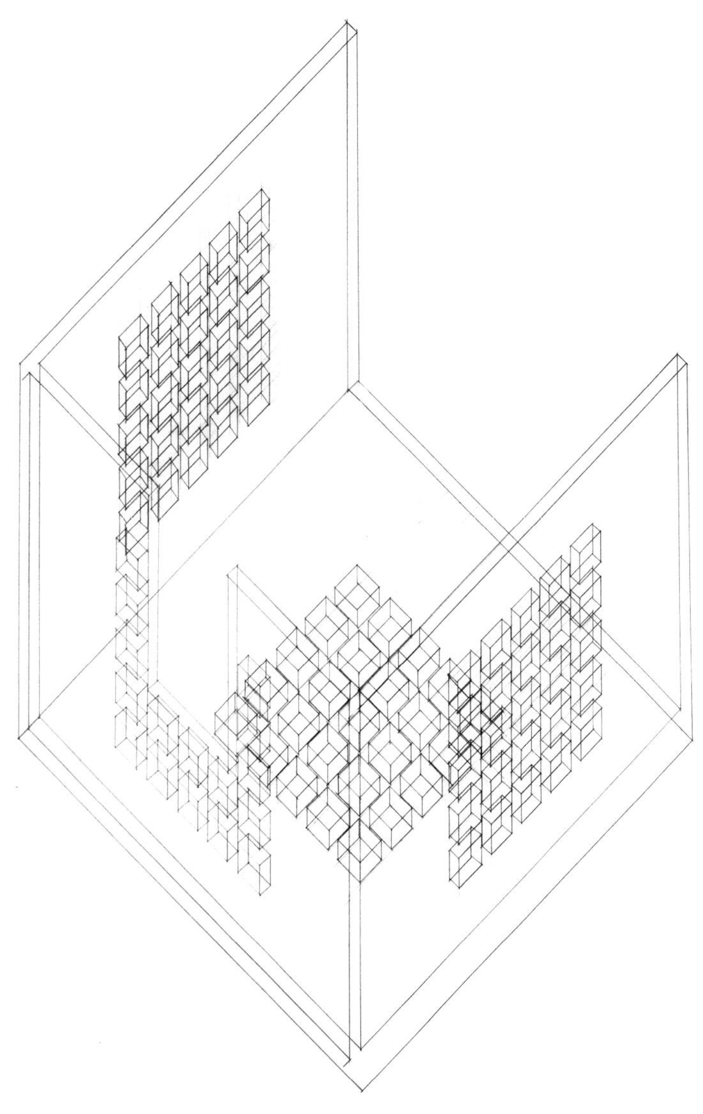

Cyclops House (open pattern), ca. 1998
graphite on vellum
Composition: 21 x 24 inches (53.3 x 61 cm)
Collection Museum of Contemporary Art San Diego
Promised gift of L.J. Cella

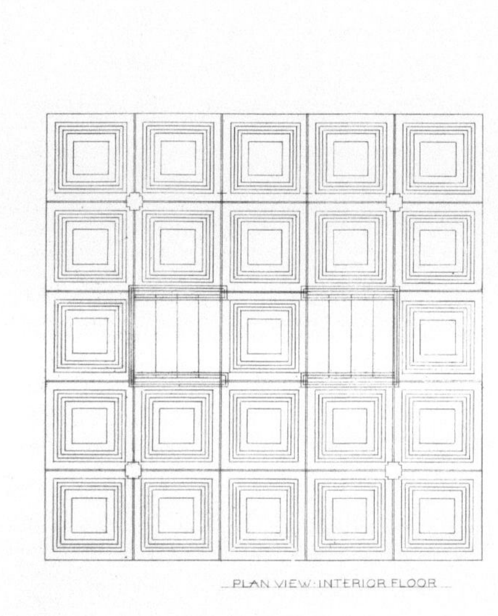

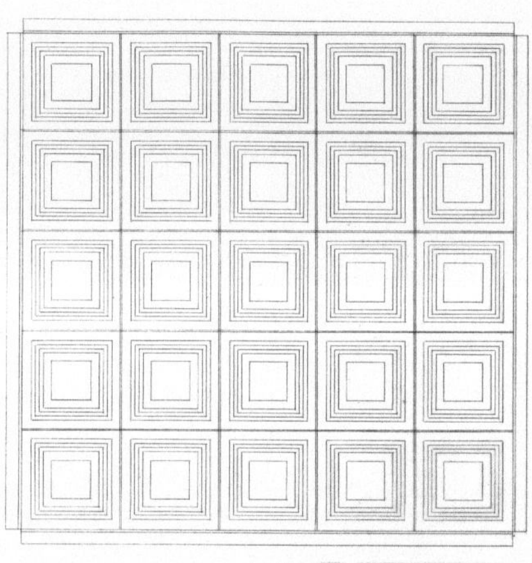

Plate 27

Cyclops House, plan and elevation, ca. 1998
graphite on vellum
Sheet: 19 x 30 inches (48.3 x 76.2 cm), each of 2
Collection Museum of Contemporary Art San Diego
Promised gift of L.J. Cella

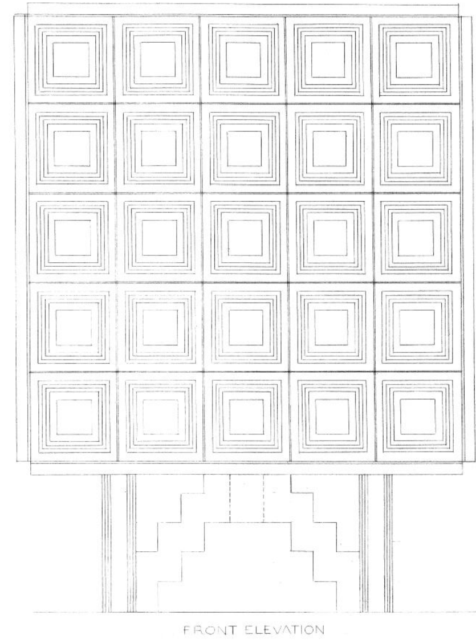

SIDE ELEVATION

FRONT ELEVATION

Plate 28

Tilt-Up Sky Space, 2001
graphite on vellum
Sheet: 16 x 42 inches (40.6 x 106.7 cm)
Collection Museum of Contemporary Art San Diego
Promised gift of L.J. Cella

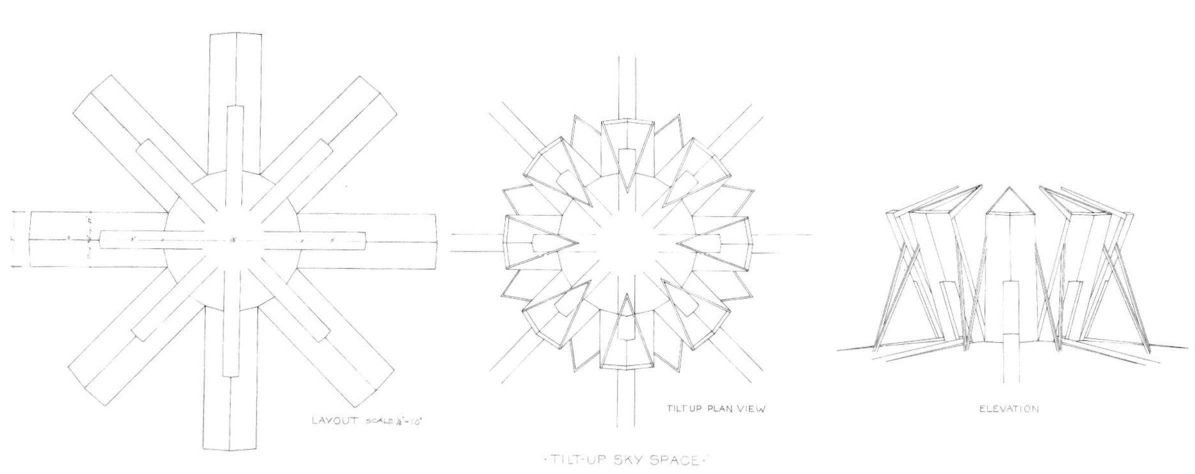

LAYOUT SCALE ⅛"=1'0"
TILT UP PLAN VIEW
ELEVATION
·TILT·UP SKY SPACE·

Plate 29

Marfa Plan, 2002
color pencil on Mylar
Sheet: 24 x 18 inches (61 x 45.7 cm)
Collection Museum of Contemporary Art San Diego
Promised gift of L.J. Cella

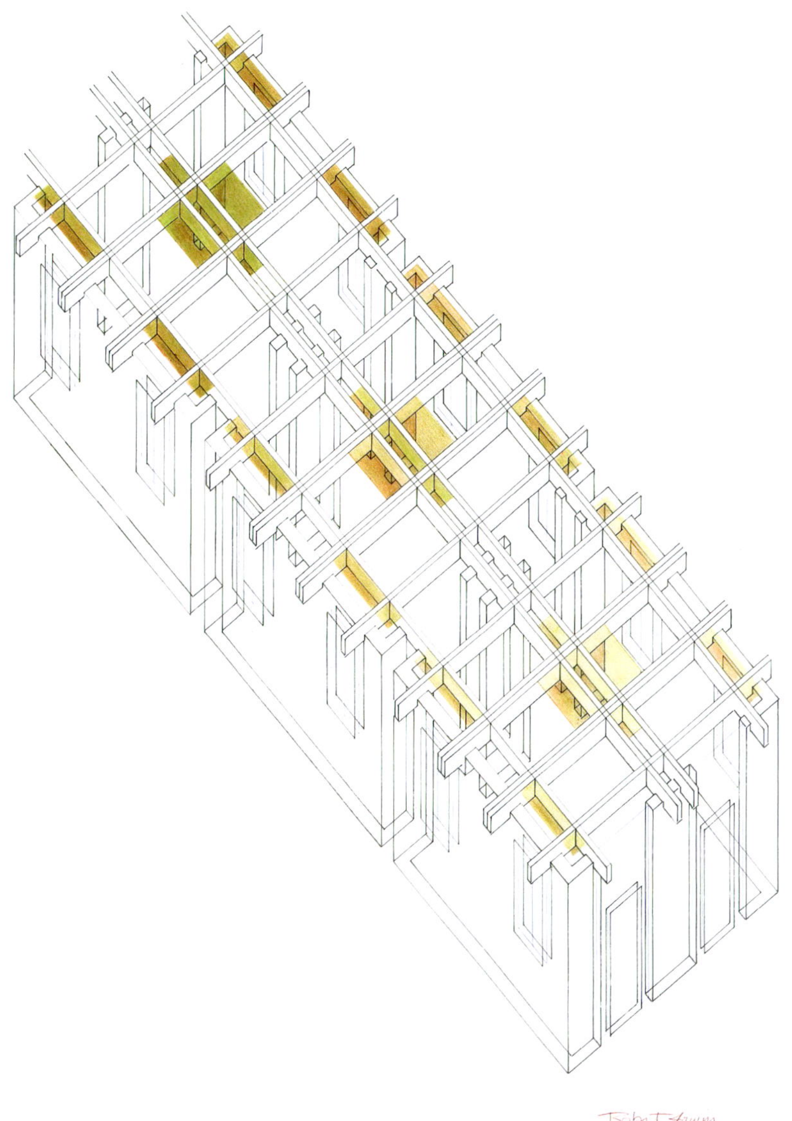

Plate 30

Marfa Color Plan, 2002
color pencil on Mylar
Sheet: 30 x 42 inches (76.2 x 106.7 cm)
Collection Museum of Contemporary Art San Diego
Promised gift of L.J. Cella

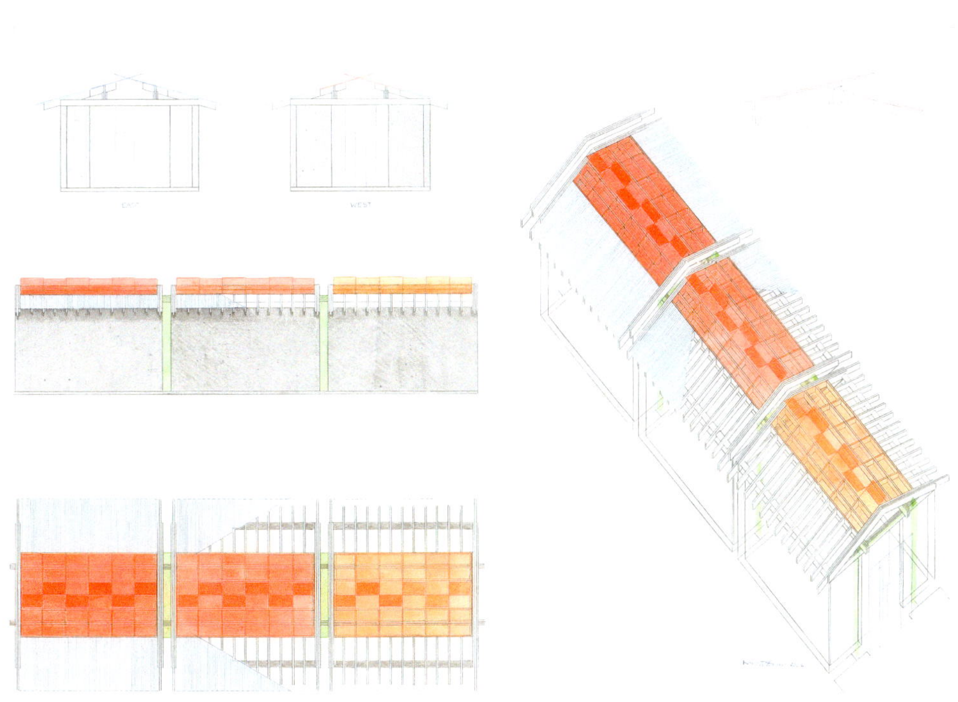

Plate 31

Marfa Plan, Elevation: South Section, 2002
color pencil and graphite on vellum
Framed: 33 3/4 x 52 1/2 x 2 inches (85.7 x 133.4 x 5.1 cm)
Collection Museum of Contemporary Art San Diego
Promised gift of L.J. Cella

EAST·WEST·ENTRANCE·EXIT·ELEVATIONS
·CONCRETE·'TILT·UP'·CONSTRUCTION·
NORTH·ELEVATION·SCALE ¼·1'0'

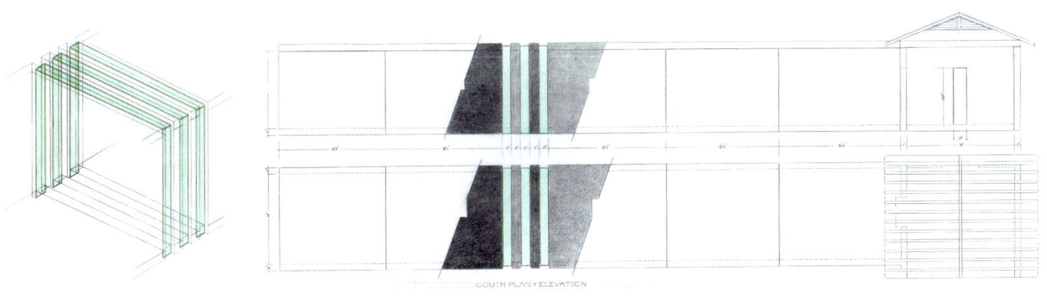
·SOUTH·PLAN·ELEVATION·

Plate 32

Color Glass (orange), Marfa Half-Plan, 2003
color pencil on Mylar
Sheet: 27 3/4 x 57 inches (70.5 x 144.8 cm)
Collection Museum of Contemporary Art San Diego
Promised gift of L.J. Cella

Plate 33

Color Glass (violet), Marfa Half-Plan, 2003
color pencil on Mylar
Sheet: 27 3/4 x 57 inches (70.5 x 144.8 cm)
Collection Museum of Contemporary Art San Diego
Promised gift of L.J. Cella

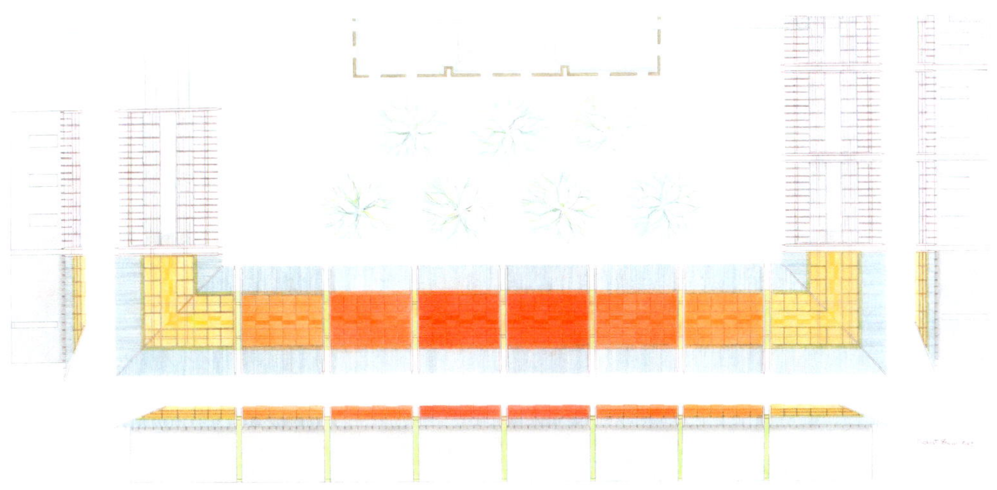

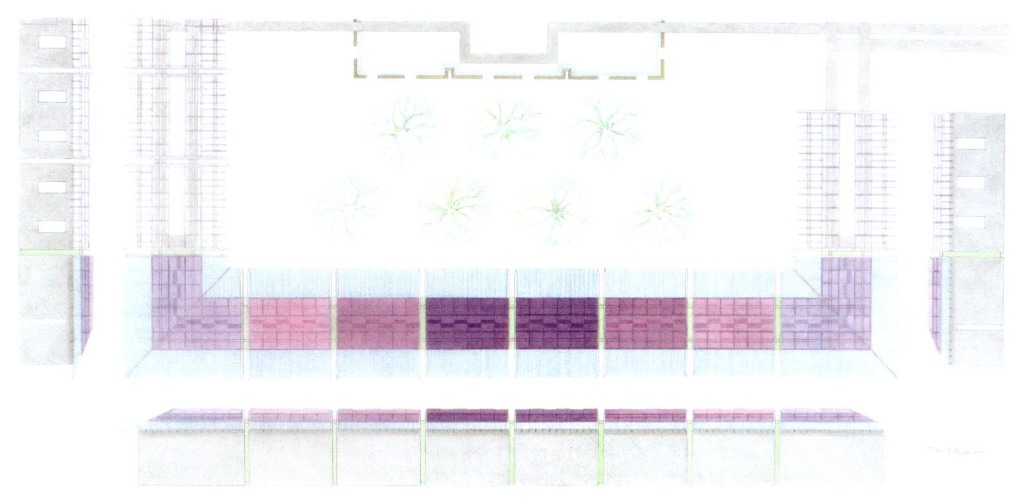

Plate 34

Marfa Plan and Elevation, 2003
graphite on Mylar
Sheet: 32 x 40 inches (81.3 x 101.6 cm)
The Collection of Deborah and Jeff Jamieson

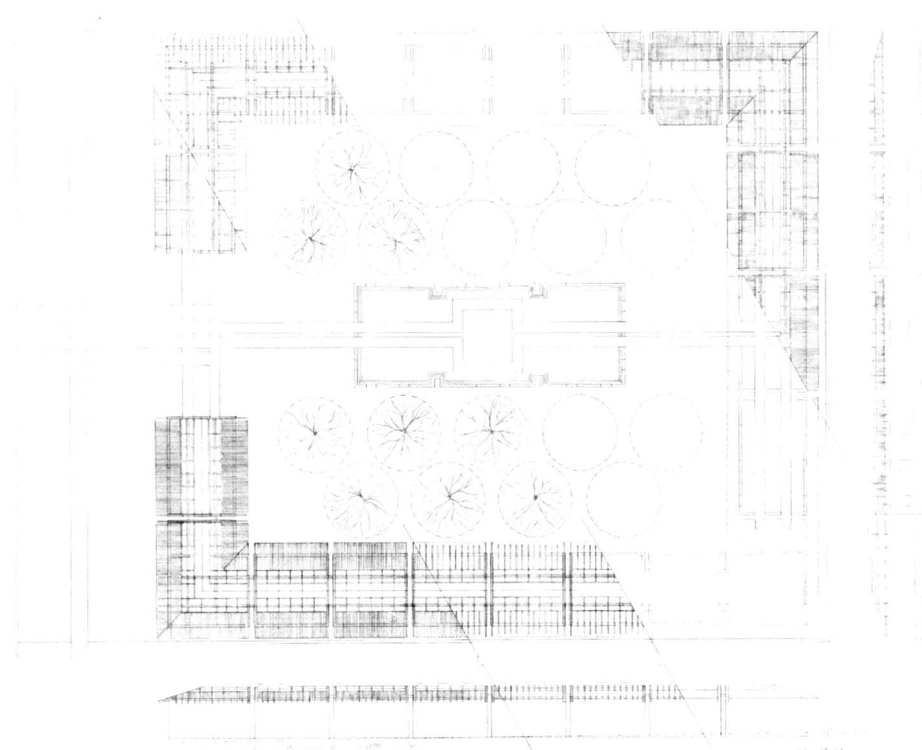

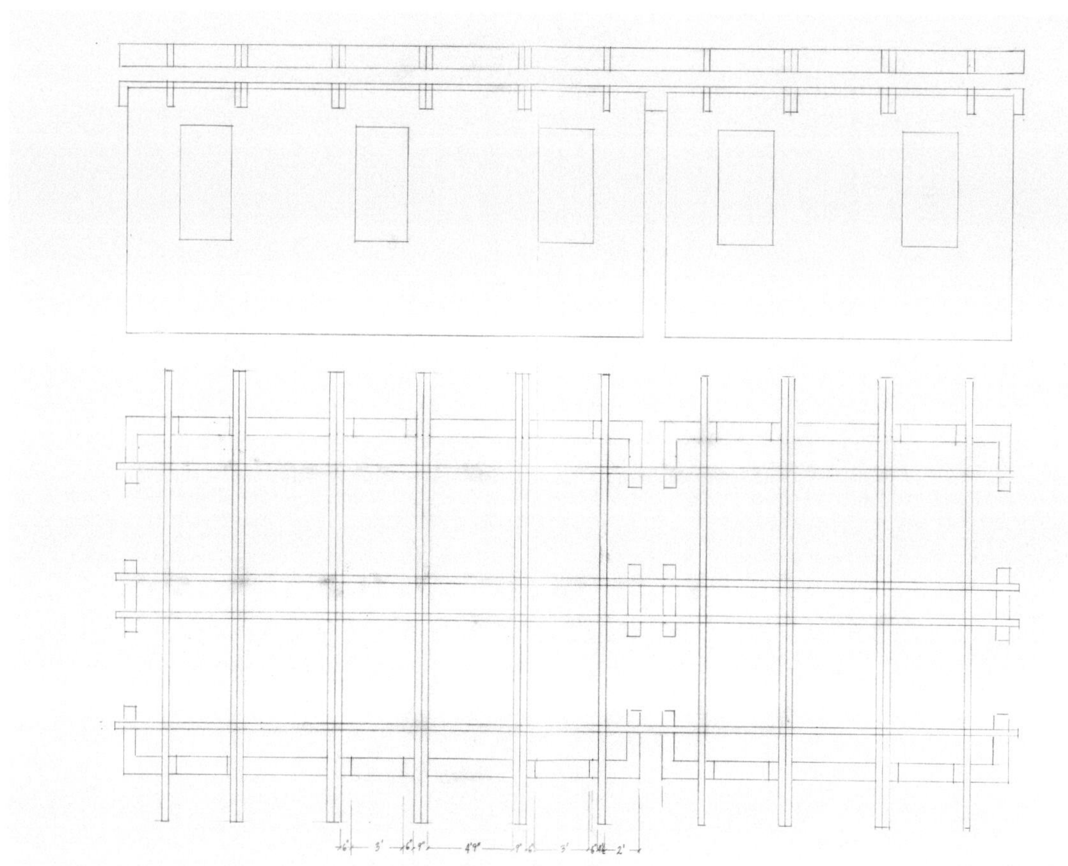

Plate 35

Irwin Marfa project, detail, 2003
graphite on Mylar
Sheet: 11 ¾ x 14 ¾ inches (29.8 x 37.5 cm)
Collection of Mark Lee and Sharon Johnston

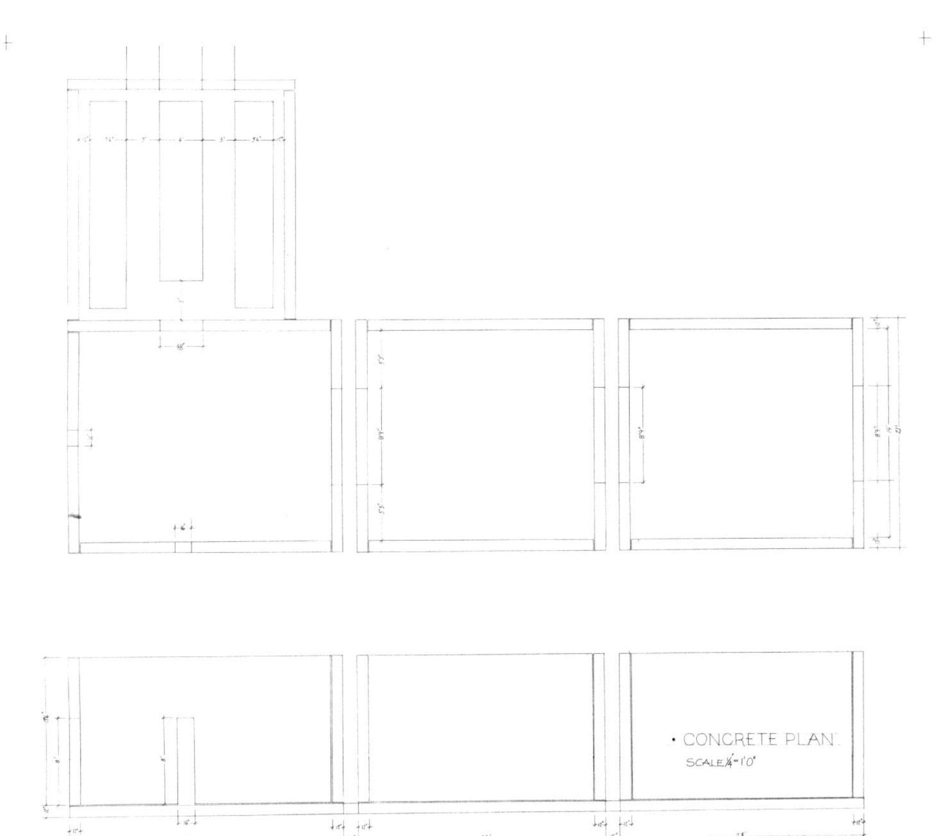

Plate 36

Irwin Marfa project, Concrete Plan, 2003
graphite on Mylar
Sheet: 25 x 19 1/2 inches (63.5 x 49.5 cm)
The Collection of Deborah and Jeff Jamieson

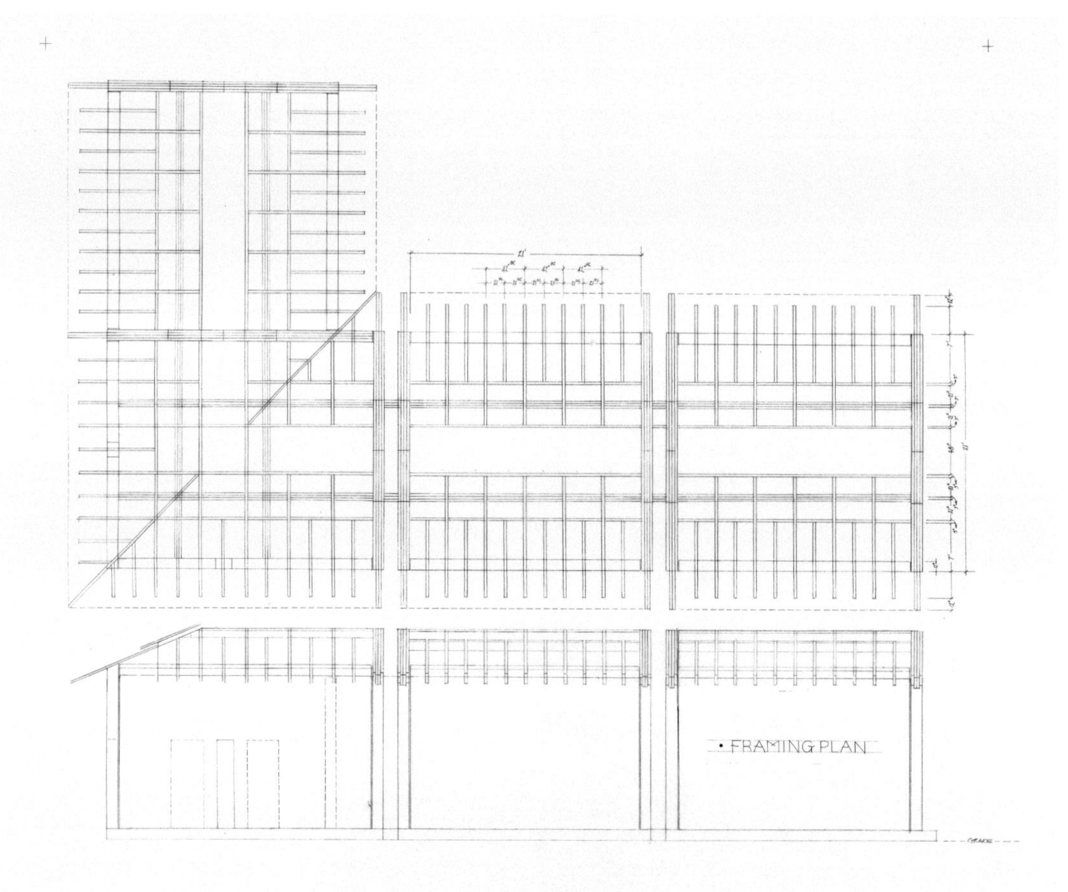

Plate 37

Irwin Marfa project, Framing Plan, 2003
graphite on Mylar
Sheet: 25 x 19 1/2 inches (63.5 x 49.5 cm)
The Collection of Deborah and Jeff Jamieson

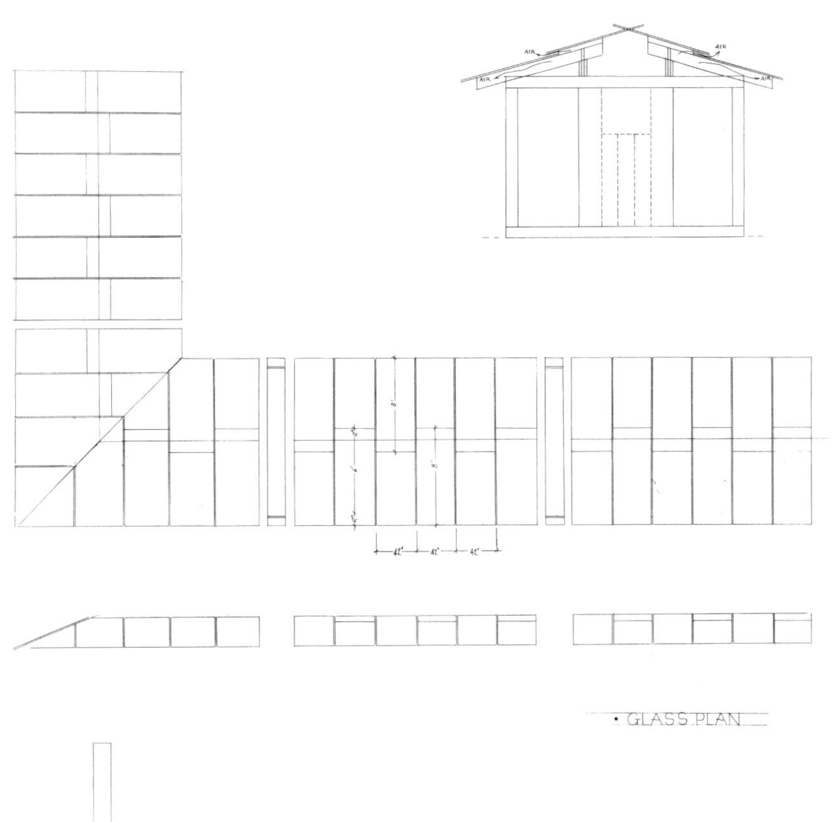

Plate 38

Irwin Marfa project, Glass Plan, 2003
graphite on Mylar
Sheet: 25 x 19 1/2 inches (63.5 x 49.5 cm)
The Collection of Deborah and Jeff Jamieson

Irwin Marfa Project, detail, 2003
clear pine wood and baltic birch plywood model
9 3/4 x 29 1/4 x 29 1/4 inches (24.8 x 74.3 x 74.3 cm)
The Chinati Foundation
Fabrication: Jeff Jamieson

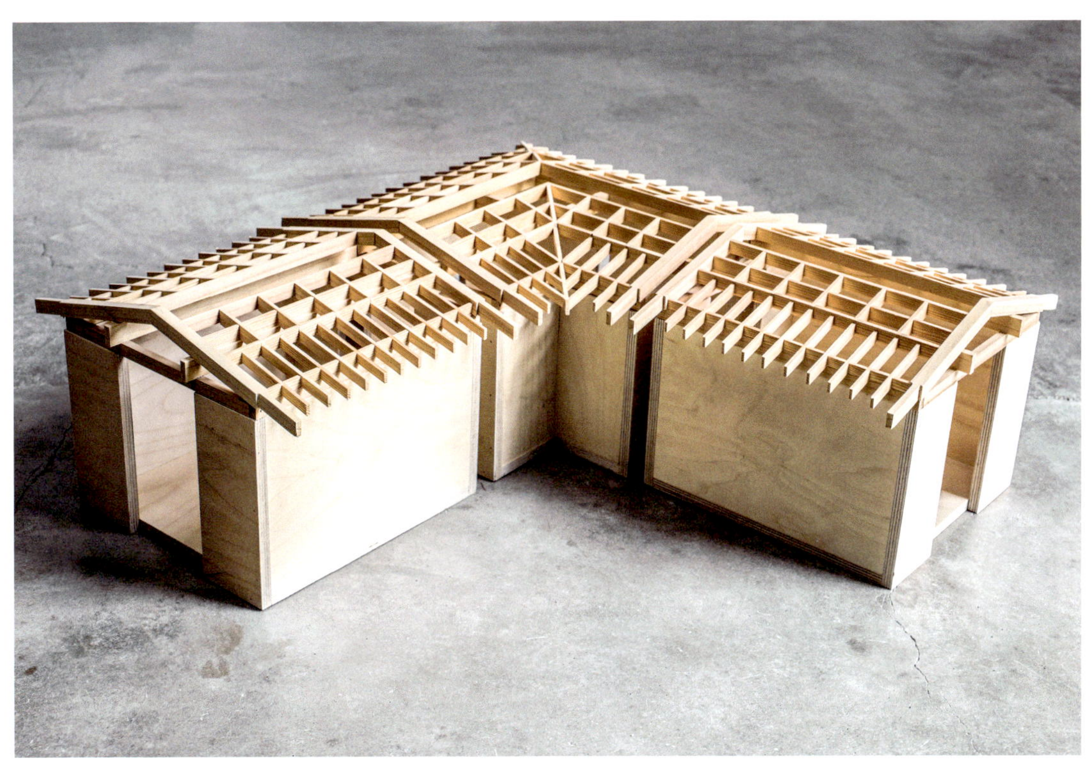

Plate 40

Marfa, details, 2004
graphite on vellum
Framed: 12 x 30 3/4 inches (30.5 x 78.1 cm)
Collection Museum of Contemporary Art San Diego
Promised gift of L.J. Cella

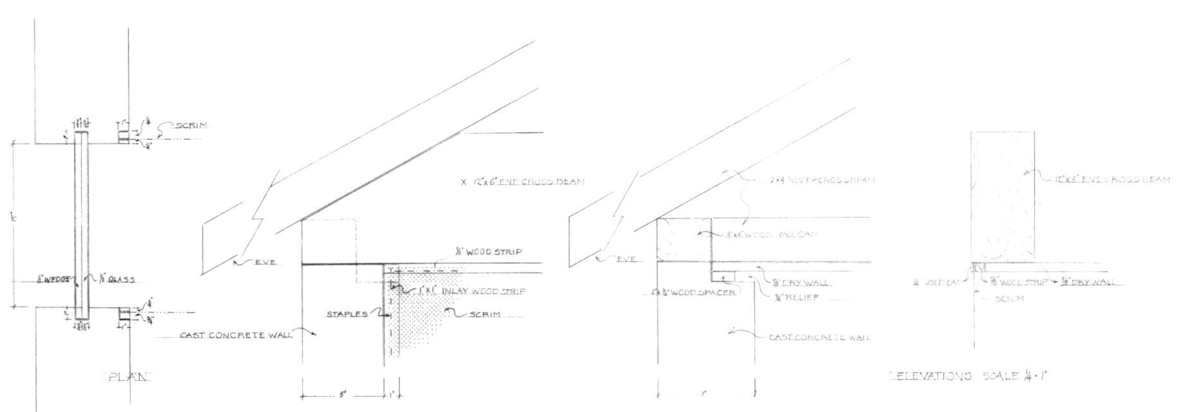

SCRIM
½" WEDGE
½" GLASS
PLAN
EVE
CAST CONCRETE WALL
STAPLES
8"
1"
X 12"x6" END CROSS BEAM
⅞" WOOD STRIP
1"x1" INLAY WOOD STRIP
SCRIM
2x4 ROOF CROSS SPAN
2"x4" WOOD WALL CAP
EVE
2"x½" WOOD SPACER
⅝" DRY WALL
¼" RELIEF
CAST CONCRETE WALL
1"
12"x6" END CROSS BEAM
¼" WOOD CAP
⅞" WOOD STRIP
⅝" DRY WALL
SCRIM
ELEVATIONS SCALE ¼"=1'

Plate 41

Marfa, details, July 2004
color pencil on paper
Framed: 18 x 26 1/2 inches (45.7 x 67.3 cm)
Collection Museum of Contemporary Art San Diego
Promised gift of L.J. Cella

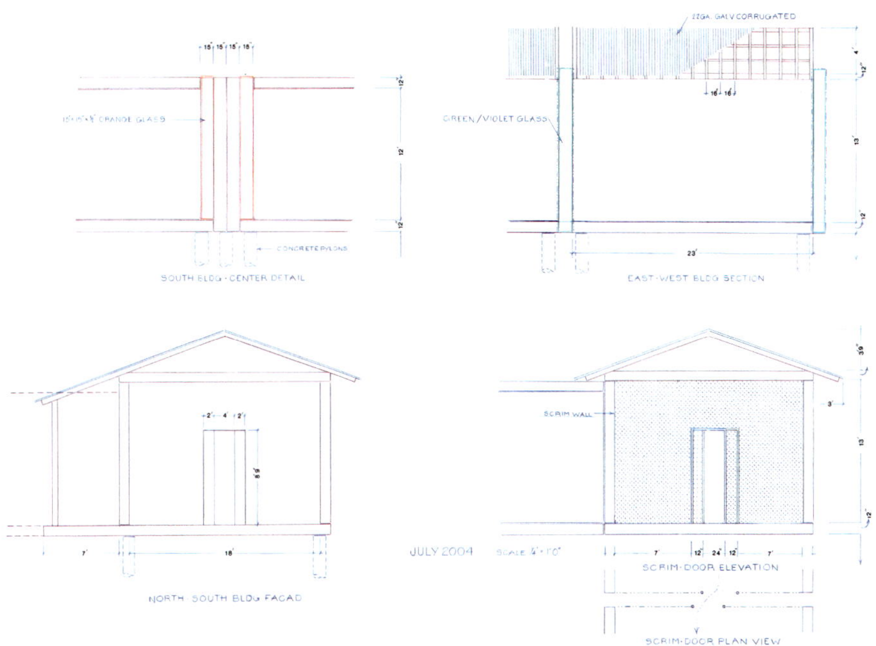
18" 18" 18" 18"
13'½" ORANGE GLASS
12'
CONCRETE PYLONS
SOUTH BLDG · CENTER DETAIL
22GA. GALV CORRUGATED
GREEN/VIOLET GLASS
16" 16"
13'
23'
EAST-WEST BLDG SECTION
2' 4' 2'
5'
7' 18'
NORTH-SOUTH BLDG FACAD
36'
SCRIM WALL
3'
13'
7' 12" 24" 12" 7'
SCRIM-DOOR ELEVATION
SCRIM-DOOR PLAN VIEW
JULY 2004   SCALE ¼" = 1'0"

Plate 42

Marfa Plan Elevations, July 2004
color pencil on Mylar
Framed: 18 x 30 inches (45.7 x 76.2 cm)
Collection Museum of Contemporary Art San Diego
Promised gift of L.J. Cella

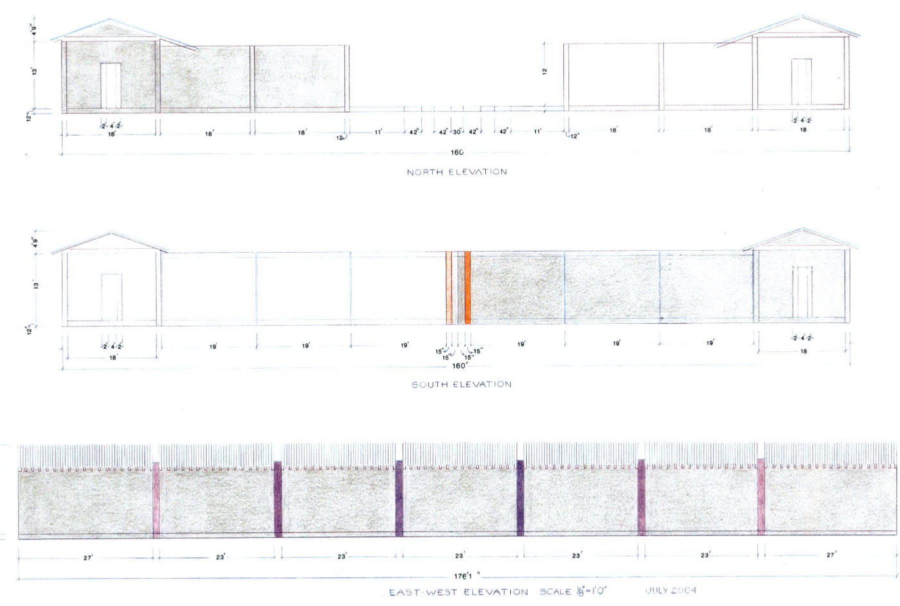

NORTH ELEVATION
SOUTH ELEVATION
EAST-WEST ELEVATION   SCALE 1/8"=1'0"   JULY 2004

Plate 43

Marfa Plan, July 2004
color pencil on Mylar
Sheet: 29 x 36 inches (73.7 x 91.4 cm)
Collection Museum of Contemporary Art San Diego
Promised gift of L.J. Cella

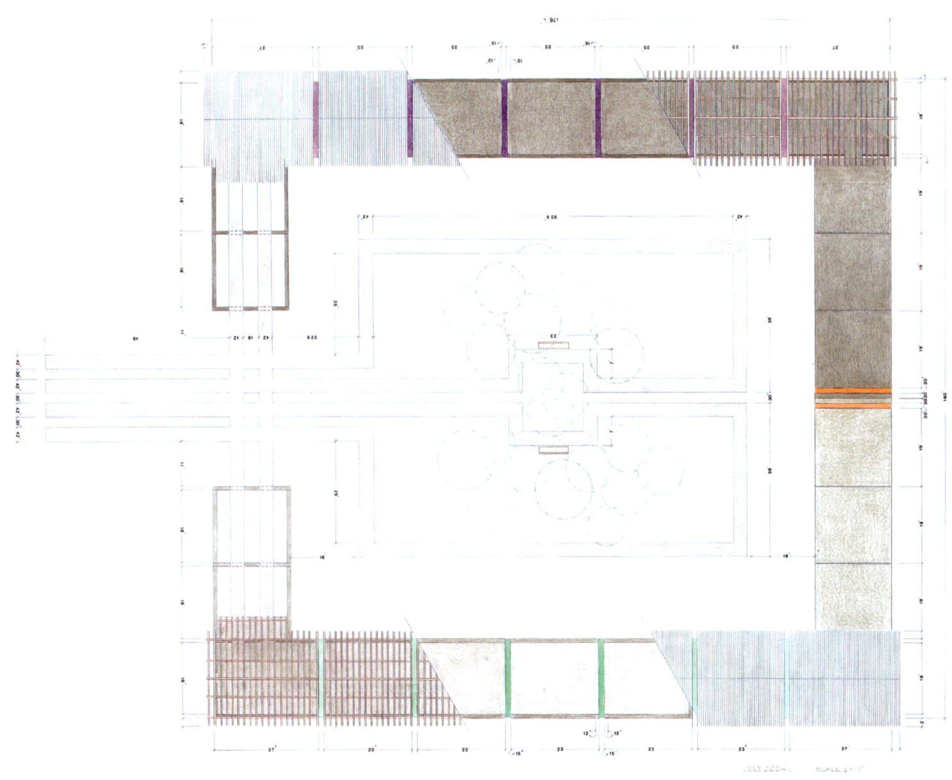

Marfa Early Plan (black & white), April 2005
graphite on paper
Framed: 30 x 36 inches (76.2 x 91.4 cm)
Collection Museum of Contemporary Art San Diego
Promised gift of L.J. Cella

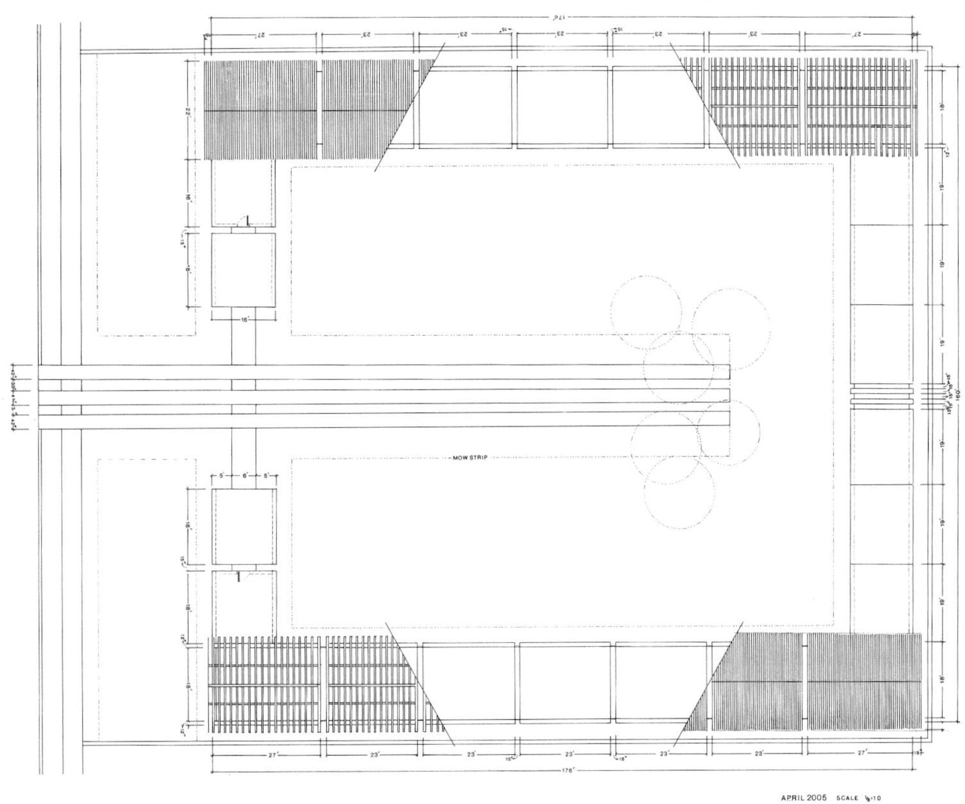

139

Plate 45

Marfa Plan (black & white), 2005–2006
graphite and color pencil on Mylar
Framed: 34 3/4 x 57 x 1 3/4 inches (88.3 x 144.8 x 4.4 cm)
Collection Museum of Contemporary Art San Diego
Promised gift of L.J. Cella

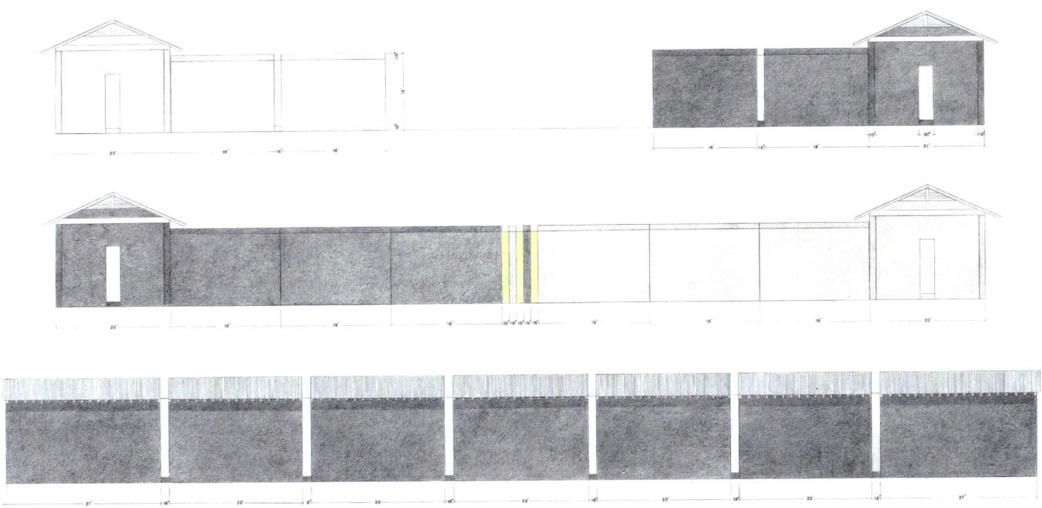

Fort D.A. Russell Hospital, Chinati Foundation, Main and Center Building Plans, 2007
graphite on Mylar
45 x 48 1/4 x 2 inches (114.3 x 122.6 x 5.1 cm)
Sheet: 36 x 40 1/2 inches (88.9 x 100.3 cm)
Collection Museum of Contemporary Art San Diego
Promised gift of L.J. Cella

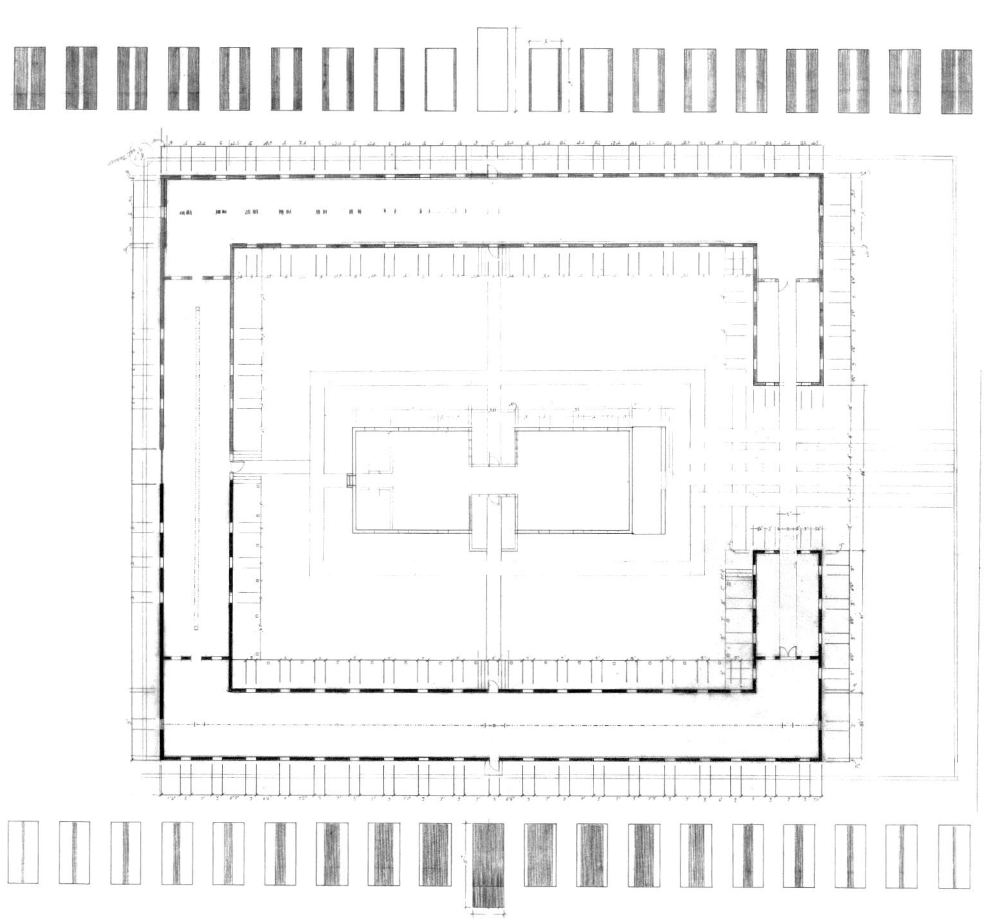

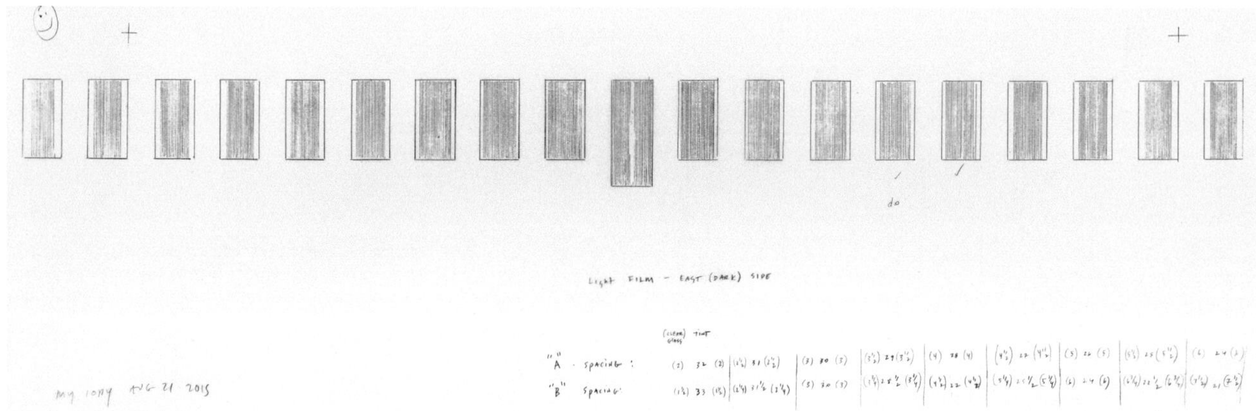

Plate 47

Irwin Marfa project, Window Mock-Up, East Wing (unrealized), 2007
graphite on Mylar
Sheet: 12 x 36 inches (30.5 x 91.4 cm)
The Collection of Deborah and Jeff Jamieson

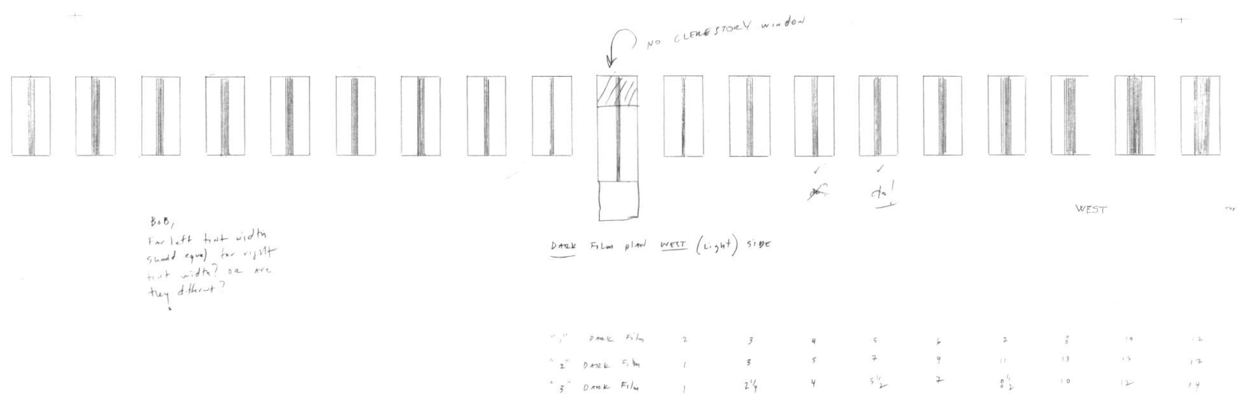

Irwin Marfa project, Window Mock-Up, West Wing (unrealized), 2007
graphite on Mylar
Sheet: 12 x 36 inches (30.5 x 91.4 cm)
The Collection of Deborah and Jeff Jamieson

145

Plate 49

Irwin Marfa Project, 2013
graphite, felt tip pen, and color pencil on Mylar
36 x 26 inches (91.4 x 66 cm)
The Chinati Foundation

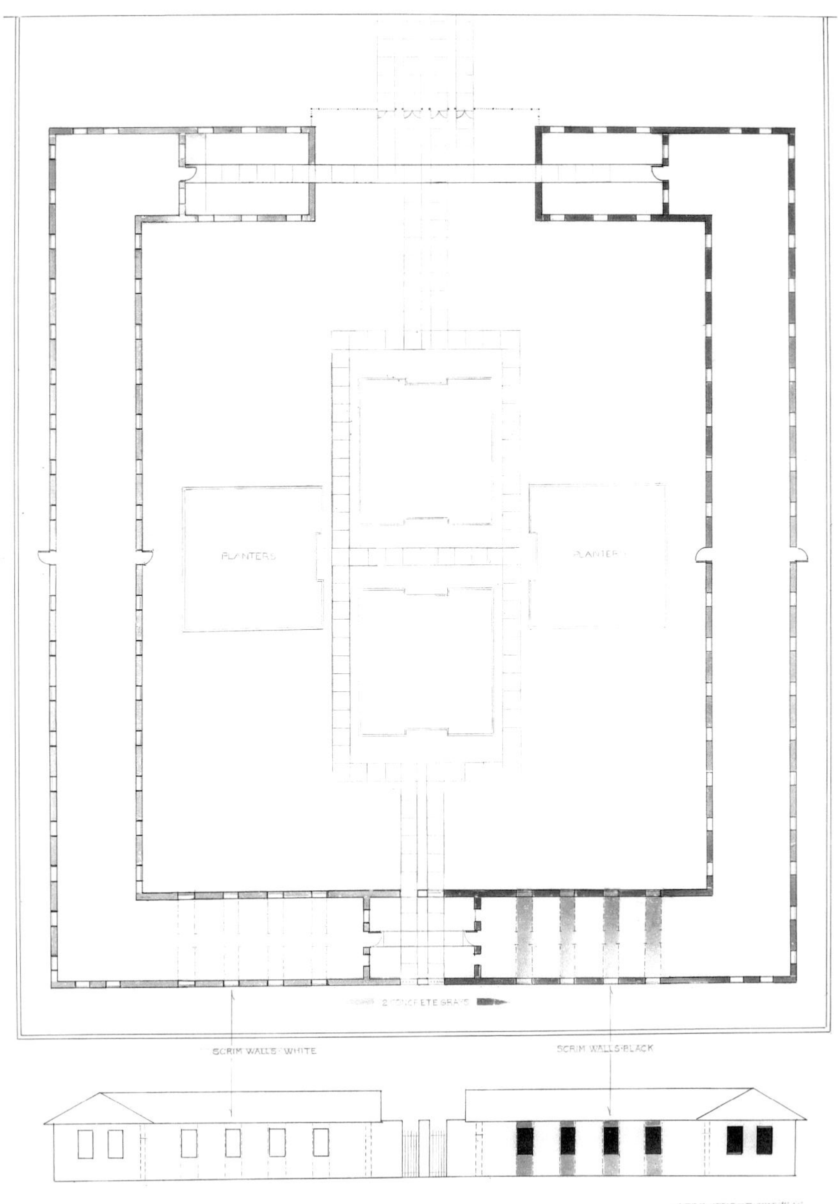

PLANTERS
PLANTER
2 CONCRETE GRAYS
SCRIM WALLS·WHITE
SCRIM WALLS·BLACK
APRIL 2013·IRWIN

Plate 50

Black on White, 2011
model
4 x 10 1/4 x 29 inches (10.2 x 26 x 73.6 cm)
Collection of the Artist

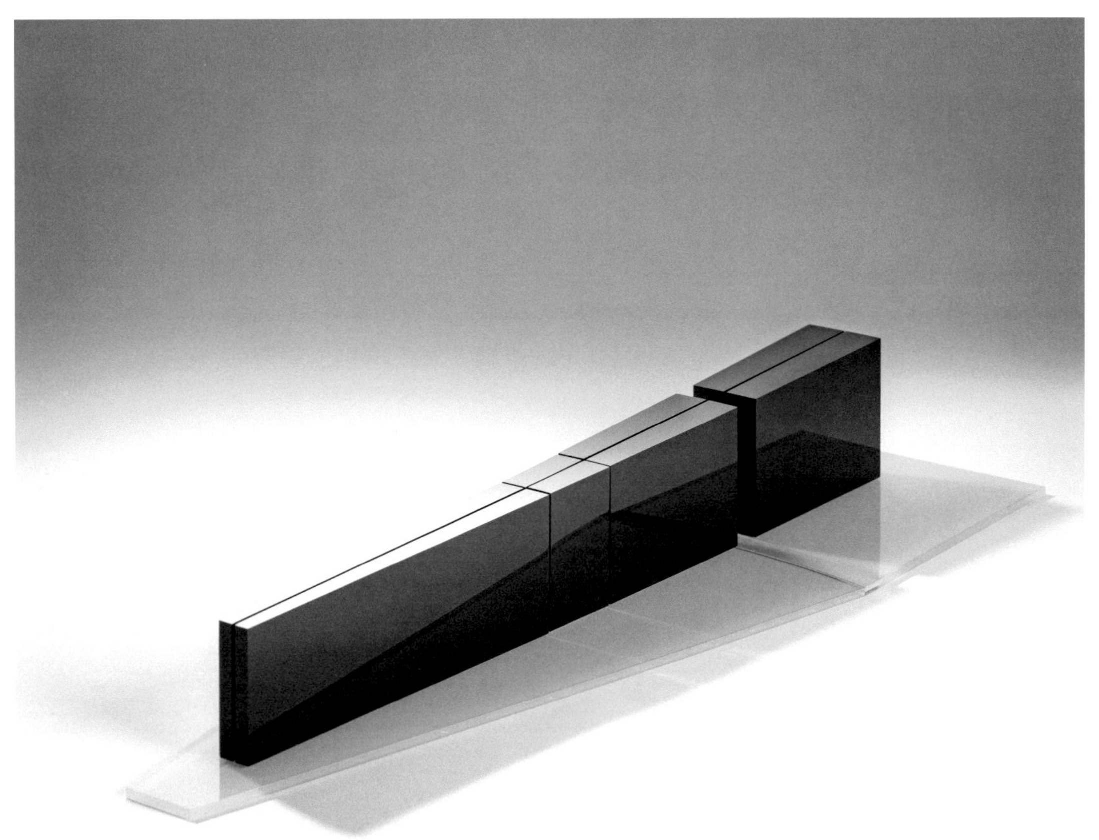

Plate 51

Black on White, 2011
color pencil and collage on Mylar
Framed: 26 1/2 x 26 3/4 x 1 7/8 inches (67.3 x 67.9 x 4.8 cm)
Sight: 18 x 19 inches (45.7 x 48.3 cm)
Collection Museum of Contemporary Art San Diego
Gift of Steven D. McIntee, 2013.109

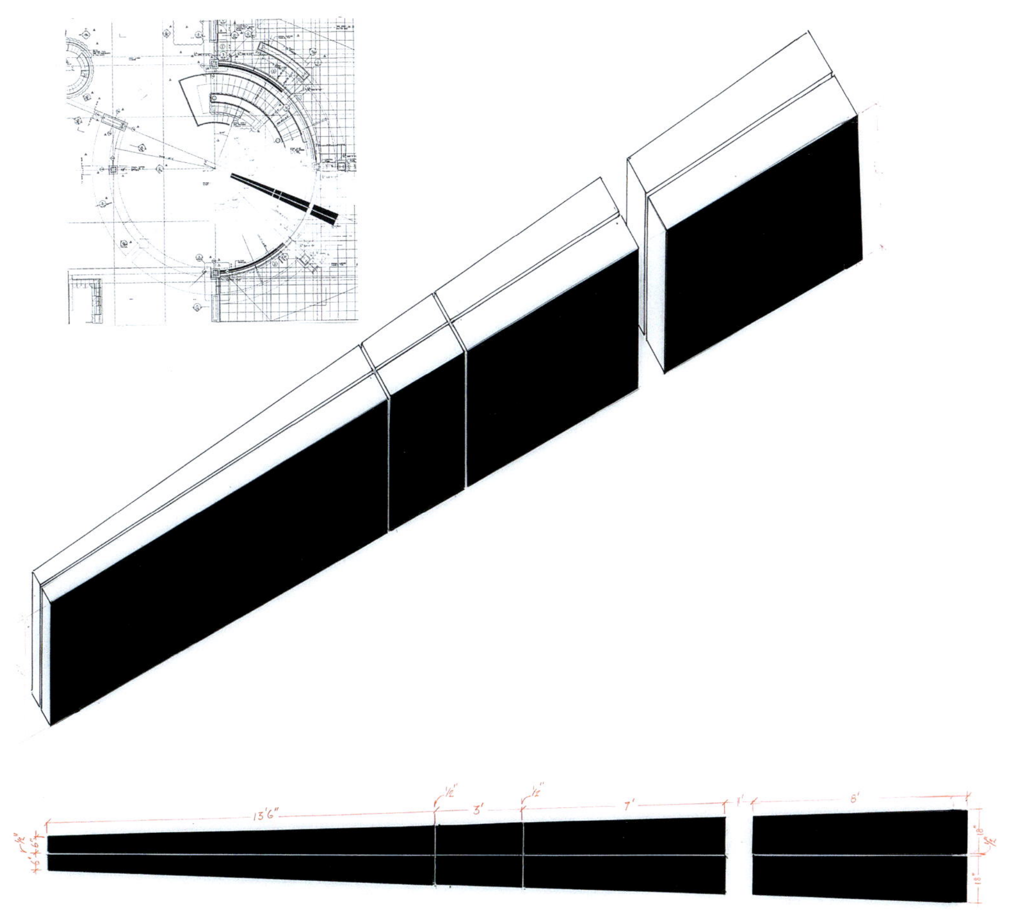

"PACIFIC STANDARD TIME" · GETTY CENTER LOBBY·

Irwin Marfa project, 2014
mixed media model: MDF, wood, acrylic, museum board and paint
5 3/8 x 47 9/16 x 55 9/16 inches (13.7 x 120.1 x 141 cm)
The Chinati Foundation
Fabrication: Ford, Powell & Carson Architects & Planners, Inc.

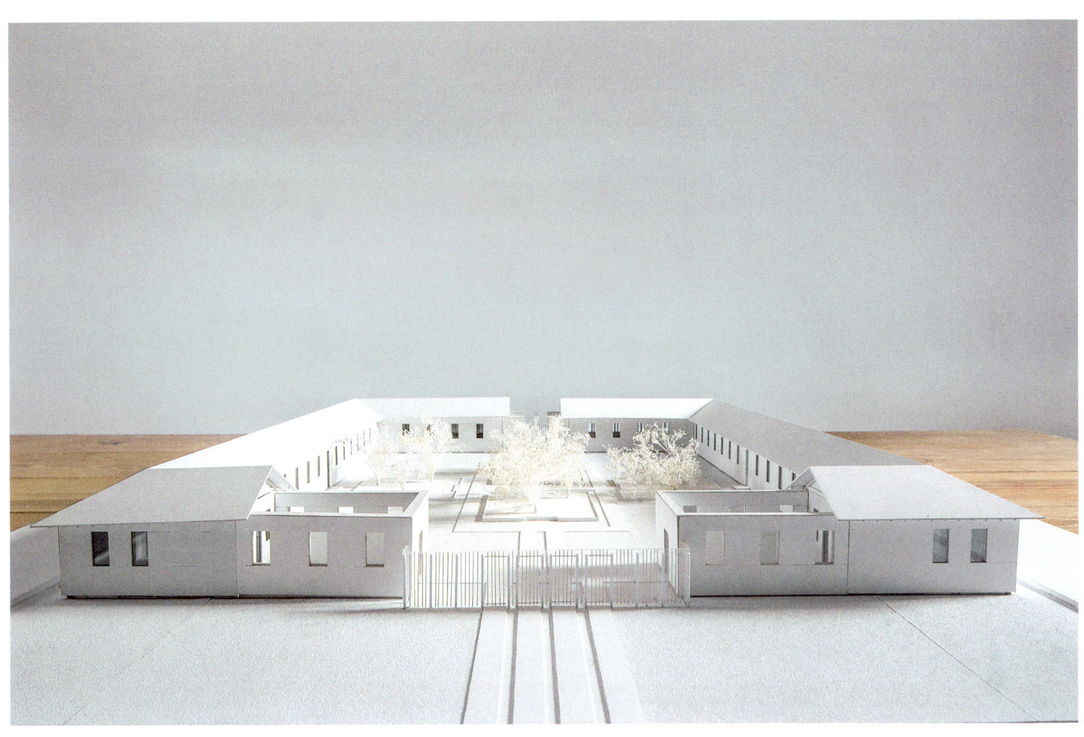

ACKNOWLEDGMENTS

Many individuals and organizations contributed to making this exhibition and catalogue possible. Our gratitude goes first to Robert Irwin, for his friendship and inspiration at all stages of this project. His *Window Wall*, located on the California State University, Long Beach (CSULB) campus, is a constant reminder that site-determined art draws its strength not from exhibitions and catalogues, but rather from the unique conditions of the places in which it is situated. We also want to thank Joseph Huppert, who offered moral support and sage advice at key moments as the exhibition took form.

We were fortunate to enjoy the generosity of individuals and institutions who lent work to the exhibition. The Museum of Contemporary Art San Diego agreed to lend over twenty drawings and three models, effectively making the exhibition viable. Thanks go to Kathryn Kanjo, Hugh Davies, Tom Callas, and Karin Zonis-Sawrey. The Getty Research Institute was the next largest institutional lender, permitting us to borrow four spectacular drawings of the Getty Central Garden. We extend our sincere gratitude to the GRI staff, especially to Thomas Gaehtgens, Andrew Perchuk, and Lora Chin Derrien. We also would like to recognize the Chinati Foundation. Jenny Moore and Rob Weiner kindly allowed us to borrow two models and a drawing for Irwin's recently completed *Untitled (dawn to dusk)*. Both the Palm Springs Art Museum and the Special Collections and Archives of the University of California, San Diego kindly lent drawings. In Palm Springs, we enjoyed the gracious support of Elena Incardona; and at UCSD, we were aided by Lynda Claassen. Individuals also generously lent work to the exhibition, including Jeff Jamieson and Deborah Denker, and Mark Lee and Sharon Johnston. Finally, Irwin allowed us to borrow three models from his studio. We are indebted to all of our lenders, both institutional and individual, for allowing us to exhibit these rarely seen drawings and models.

We wish to recognize University Art Museum Director Kimberli Meyer, and to thank her for her support of this project, as well as the thoughtful remarks that appear at the outset of this publication. UAM Associate Director Brian Trimble rallied enthusiasm for the project and secured the financial support needed to make it a reality. And, Pet Sourinthone guided the exhibition design and didactic materials. It is to Maria Coltharp, however, that I personally owe my greatest debt of gratitude. Maria oversaw the exhibition from the beginning, including managing the exhibition catalogue. Her good humor and professionalism were essential to navigating the project through all its many twists and turns. Sally Yard and Ed Schad contributed outstanding essays to this catalogue, shedding new light on Irwin's site-determined art (Ellen Thornton expertly copyedited the texts). We are grateful to Mary DelMonico, Anne Wu, and Karen Farquhar of DelMonico Books•Prestel for producing a beautiful catalogue. Andrew Byrom masterfully designed the catalogue in a way that respects and extends the aesthetics of the exhibited work. For their assistance securing images and permissions, we thank Nilofar Babazadeh, Elizabeth Christopher, Helen Connor, Rutger Fuchs, Florian Holzherr, Jennifer Lees, Jessica Lutz, Halle Mares, Alex Marks, Lindsay McGuire, Jason Meintjes, Virginia Mokslaveskas, Julia Murphy, Emily Park, Amanda Sanfilippo, Tracey Schuster, and William Vizcarra. We are especially grateful to Philipp Scholz Rittermann, whose inspiring photographs helped make this catalogue a powerful visual document.

We would like to extend a heartfelt thank you to those who generously provided financial support to this enterprise. Exhibition and publication funding was granted by the Contemporary Collectors of Orange County, the Pasadena Art Alliance, the Graham Foundation, and the Port of Long Beach. Additional support was provided by the Museum Studies Program at the CSULB College of the Arts; the CSULB Instructionally Related Activities Fund; CSULB Associate Students, Inc.; the Ware Endowment; the Charles and Elizabeth Brooks Endowment; the Constance W. Glenn Fund for Exhibition and Education Programs; the Arts Council for Long Beach; and Dr. Ronald and Sylvia Hartman.

Many individuals and friends also deserve recognition for their often-intangible contributions to making this exhibition and catalogue a reality. I wish to single out Jeffrey Ryan, who advised me on the exhibition concept as it evolved and provided feedback as it picked up steam. Others who have my gratitude are Michael Armstrong, Mary Beebe, Margaret Black, Kendall Brown, L.J. Cella, Lolotte Cholette, Evelyn Hankins, Cooper Jamieson, Karen Kleinfelder, Sanford Kwintner, Harmony Murphy, Cyrus Parker-Jeannette, Rachel Rivenc, Roger Rothman, Mark Ruwedel, Peter Stanley, Marianne Stockebrand, and Nick Terry. I would also like to thank the students in my Spring 2017 undergraduate seminar, especially Gabriel Avalos, Athena Diego, and Christian Morales, for stimulating discussions about the concept of the exhibition. Last but not least, I wish to express my love and gratitude to my family—Florence, Andrew, and Gabriel—for their excitement about this project from start to finish.

All images © 2018 Robert Irwin / Artists Rights Society (ARS), New York
and courtesy of the artist unless otherwise noted.

Essay Image Credits

Courtesy of the University Art Museum, California State University, Long Beach
Pages 16; 18, left; 63

Jan Butterfield Papers, Archives of American Art, Smithsonian Institution, Washington, DC
Pages 18, right; 19

Lee Stalsworth
Page 20

Courtesy of the Ohio State University
Page 22, bottom

Philipp Scholz Rittermann
Pages 25; 39; 41, left; 41, right; 42; 44; 55, right; 56; 57; 58; 59; cover images

Courtesy of Pace Gallery
Page 28

© J. Paul Getty Trust
Pages 35, 36

© Hemis / Alamy Stock Photo
Page 38

Ed Schad
Page 50

© Luc Novovitch / Alamy Stock Photo
Page 51

Donald Judd Art © 2018 Judd Foundation / Artists Rights Society (ARS), New York
Page 52, left

Florian Holzherr
Page 52, right

Courtesy of the Chinati Foundation
Pages 53; 55, left

William Vizcarra
Page 54

Exhibition Checklist Photography and Image Credits

Matthew Fukushima
Plate 1

Lance Gerber Studio
Plate 2

Pablo Mason
Plates 3; 6–17; 24–33; 40–46; 51

Philipp Scholz Rittermann
Plates 4–5; 20; 23; 50

Courtesy of the Getty Research Institute
Plates 18–19

© J. Paul Getty Trust
Plates 21 and 22

Deborah Denker
Plates 34; 36–38; 47–48

Jason Meintjes
Plate 35

Alex Marks
Plates 39; 49; 52

Cover: Detail of *Two Running Violet V Forms*, 1982 (Plate 4)
Back Cover: Detail of *Two Running Violet V Forms*, 1982 (Page 25)